EAST INTO YESTERDAY

AN OMF BOOK

© OVERSEAS MISSIONARY FELLOWSHIP
(formerly China Inland Mission)

Published by
Overseas Missionary Fellowship (IHQ) Ltd.,
2 Cluny Road, Singapore 1025, Republic of Singapore

First published 1990

OMF BOOKS are distributed by
OMF, 404 South Church Street, Robesonia, Pa 19551, USA
OMF, Belmont, The Vine, Sevenoaks, Kent, TN13 3TZ, UK
OMF, P O Box 849, Epping, NSW 2121, Australia
OMF, 1058 Avenue Road, Toronto, Ontario M5N 2C6, Canada
OMF, P O Box 10159 Balmoral, Auckland, New Zealand
OMF, P O Box 41, Kenilworth 7745, South Africa
and other OMF offices.

ISBN 9971-972-94-8

Printed in Singapore
SK SW 9/90

Contents

Contents

Is this a true story? Well, yes and no. The people you'll meet are very real people. The events in which they are involved actually happened. Whether Jeff and his friend Wu Liang are real — well, that's up to you.

ONE

Uncle Zeke's Project

Jeff Anderson peered out the side window of the station wagon as it merged into the traffic along the Illinois expressway. Rain trickled into crooked patterns down the window, blurring the image of the car in the next lane. The steel sky formed a heavy ceiling, blocking out the skyscrapers Jeff knew towered just ahead. *Wouldn't you know it, first day of Spring break and it rains! Some vacation!* Much as he liked Aunt Nonie and Uncle Zeke, a family visit to their home in Batavia, Illinois wasn't exactly thrilling, even on the brightest of days. With rain for a whole week it would be really grim.

He turned the pages of the game book he'd been working on. "Fill in the blanks below to find your future", it said. He began to answer the questions. "Color of your hair?" He wrote, "dark brown". "Your age?" He filled in "14". "Weight?" *One hundred twenty seven — a little too much for his height, but it was the truth. Besides it was all solid.* "Your grade in school:" *nine.* "Now add the numbers above and divide by three. If the total ..."

Phooey with that. He closed the book, restlessly. It was hard to concentrate anyway over the high-pitched beeps of the video game his younger brother, Greg, held in his hand. At ten years old, Greg could be fairly intelligent company, or could drive Jeff crazy.

"What are we going to do this week anyway?" he asked, raising his voice so his Dad could hear.

Mr Anderson glanced at Jeff in the rear view mirror. "I know that one day while we're there Zeke'll take us to see his work at Fermi Lab. That'll be interesting. You know," he said slowly, emphasizing each word, "Fermi Lab is the biggest particle accelerator in the world."

Jeff said nothing. What was so exciting about a "particle accelerator"? Not that he hadn't heard of it before. But on a scale from one to ten, physics would rate a low three when it came to interests. "If we're going to have to look at it, I wish he had a more exciting job," he told his dad. "Like you. I like spending a day watching you in surgery or making rounds with you in the cardiac care unit like I did that time. That was interesting. But a particle accelerator? Uh-uh."

Well, it'd probably be worth an hour or two of his time even though he could think of better ways to spend his spring break.

They traveled on a few minutes in silence. Silence, that is, except for the intermittent electronic whine of Greg's game. "I hope it isn't going to rain like this all week, and spoil our whole vacation," Jeff muttered.

"Just pretend you're going to Bermuda, or Acapulco, or the Riviera or somewhere warm like that. Think sand, sun, surf ..."

"Yeeeeaahh," Jeff drawled, folding his arms under his head. "Now you're talking. Hey, remember last Thursday when I opened my fortune cookie?"

"Yeah," Greg said, suddenly interested. "I got 'you will meet a person of great influence who will help you succeed.' I'm looking for him — or her. Maybe Uncle Zeke will introduce me to some of his smart scientific friends and it'll come true."

"It'd take more than that to help you succeed," Jeff said, laughing as he lunged at his brother in a playful attack.

"Oh, yeah?" Greg said, wrestling his way out of the headlock Jeff held him in.

"Anyway, there's nothing to the stuff you read in fortune cookies. It's just made up by some typist in a cookie office in ... in California or wherever they make 'em. She makes up whatever she thinks sounds good, something vague usually, so you can't pin it down."

"I know that. D'you think I believe the stupid things? It's just fun, that's all. While you're waiting for Dad to finish his fifteenth cup of green tea!"

Jeff laughed at the reminder. "Like I was going to say, mine said something like, 'An exotic adventure will soon be yours.'" He wiped the condensation off the window beside him. "This is my 'exotic adventure'— five days in Illinois looking at a massive physics experiment?"

Mom smiled. "Hey, hold on, this might not be exotic, but look on it as an adventure and you might be surprised."

"I hope so."

When the car eventually pulled into the driveway of Zeke and Nonie's townhouse it was Andy who came bounding out the door to meet them. Four-year-old, smart-as-a-whip, always-had-an-answer-ready Andy could be counted on to liven up the visit. He chattered and questioned and followed Jeff around admiringly.

By the time they'd been there a couple of hours the rain had stopped and the sun was making every effort to penetrate the gloom. This was all the encouragement Zeke needed to suggest taking everybody down to Fermi Lab to see his work.

Jeff caught his dad's eye and returned his wink.

"Biggest cyclotron of its kind in the world," Zeke was saying. "Stretches for fifty miles in a giant circle underground. Fascinating to think of its potential."

"For what? Are you making nuclear bombs?" Greg asked.

"No, no, nothing like that." They grabbed their jackets and headed for the car and Zeke kept up the explanation as they drove.

"Actually, to put it simply, the cyclotron's a big microscope, allowing us to see not only into the atom, but more than that, right into the nucleus. By separating the protons out of that nucleus and spinning them at super speeds, which it allows us to do, we can study them and do all sorts of experiments. And we provide resources for scientists from all over the world to come and work."

Jeff wasn't too sure he understood but he nodded anyway. He knew that atoms had a nucleus made up of protons and neutrons. Now it seemed they were splitting these protons into little bits, something no one had been able to do without such high speeds. Whatever good that was.

"So what actually do *you* do?" Jeff asked.

"Well, my work is a little different from most. And this is why I'm so excited, Nat," he said looking over his shoulder to Mr Anderson. "I personally am working on a project with the code name 'Time Trek'. Sort of an experiment with time-space."

"Time-space? The fourth dimension? Isn't that just made up for science-fiction writers?" Jeff felt interest rising quickly now.

"No, not at all. Many physicists work with the concept of relativity, causality ... such things. Einstein started it all so you can blame him!" Uncle Zeke really seemed excited about what he did. He let go of the steering wheel with one hand so he could gesture as he talked.

"It's hard to explain. See, we know that as you move faster, time moves slower. If we move particles around fast enough — like here we can whirl them at astronomical speeds for extended periods — they live longer. Their 'clock' slows down. The faster they move, the slower their 'clock' goes."

"So you move them fast enough and it'll go backwards, right?" Jeff prodded.

"Weeee ... lll ..."

"Hey, does that mean if people could travel at supersonic speeds we would get younger?"

"Only in theory. If you could do it for light years."

"How 'bout that? I can see it all now, 'Scientists discover cure for aging.'"

Uncle Zeke laughed and shook his head. "No, I'm afraid not. It doesn't work that way. Anyway high velocity isn't the only thing that has that result. Gravitational pull slows time too. In fact intense gravitational force stops time." He slapped one hand on the steering wheel. "That reminds me, I asked Bill to get the crew to see if they could adjust the gravitational-density selector. I hope he did it. Seems to have a short in it somewhere." They drove off the main road past some farms to find a number of assorted buildings spread around a lake. Uncle Zeke followed the drive to the parking lot, talking as he drove.

"This is a very simplistic explanation I'm giving you, mind you. There are a lot more factors involved. For instance, ever heard of 'black holes'?"

Jeff and Greg nodded.

"Black holes are sort of holes in space, and therefore holes in time — you might think of them as holes in the big sheet called 'space-time'. The gravity is so strong in black holes, even light can't escape."

They were entering a tall concrete building whose sides sloped up in two towers. The elevator whisked them up to the 15th floor. "My office is down the hall." Jeff stepped up his pace to match his uncle's near run.

"Oh, Zeke." A grey-haired man stuck his head out of a doorway as they passed. "I had Bruce look at your GDS last night. He thinks he found the problem."

"Great. Is it fixed?"

"Yup. Just a wiring snafu."

"Thanks, Bill." Zeke resumed his stride. "Now,

as I was saying. Strong gravity stops time. Theoretically, a particle could actually be shot through space-time, into this hole in space-time, and out the other side again into the past without any changes — if high-enough speeds could be obtained."

"Wow! Then, if you could go fast enough you could go backwards or forwards in time, right?" Jeff asked, eyes widening. "You mean time-travel might really be possible after all?"

"Well, theoretically, yes. Possible. Maybe." Uncle Zeke's tone of voice was intended to put a damper on Jeff's mounting curiosity.

Jeff ignored it and continued, "And if this 'space-time' is one unit, you'd be traveling in space too, so you could go ... say, north and land in the next century, or maybe, east into ... yesterday."

Uncle Zeke shook his head. "Don't get your hopes up. No one's going to take off for the year 2070 or backwards to 20 BC or something. Not in our lifetime anyway. But as you can see, it opens up fascinating possibilities."

They entered a huge room filled with interesting machines like a futuristic movie set. Zeke led them over to a small cubicle that perched on the end of a metal arm. The steel arm was about eight inches wide and four feet long and was anchored to a motor-like box at one end, allowing it to rotate. The metal cubicle at the other end looked something like a flight simulator. Zeke gave it a push with his hand and it swung smoothly around on its base.

"Hey, this thing spins as well as the whole arm spinning! Wow! Like those saucer rides at the fair last summer! What a ride!"

"This 'ride', this chamber or cockpit here, is our gravitational-velocity module or GVM," Zeke said proudly. "You've seen how the Air Force tests the effects of gravitational pull on pilots of ultra-high-speed aircraft? Well, this is something like that. Same idea at least."

Jeff stuck his head in the little metal cubicle. When the heavy padded metal door closed, the compartment would be only big enough for one person. A swivel seat faced panels of lights that stretched all across the front like a plane's cockpit. On the screens messages were flashing constantly for anyone who wanted to decipher them. Levers, charts, buttons, dials and cords filled every inch of space.

Zeke talked for a while about things Jeff didn't understand, like "tachyons" and "singularities associated with rotation". Dad seemed to be understanding. Or at least pretending he did, Jeff decided.

Then the scientist turned to Jeff and motioned toward the experiment booth. "Why don't you go ahead and climb in the GVM and do a little experiment? I'll tell you what to do. You can't do anything too drastic. All you'll feel is a bit of pressure against you, and you'll spin around

a few times — you can choose your own angle
and altitude and direction. Then it'll stop and you
get out."

Jeff hesitated. He glanced at his dad and back
at his uncle.

"Just a spin or two; don't be afraid," Zeke
urged.

Jeff shrugged and sat down in front of the
keyboards.

"I hope this is OK. I mean, I don't know anything
about this at all. What if I press some wrong
button and end up on the moon?"

"You can't. It has nothing to do with the moon,"
Dad laughed. "China maybe, but not the moon."

"Hey, maybe this is my 'exotic adventure',"
Jeff suggested, grinning. "Here goes."

"OK. Turn your speed selector here. That's
right. Now, choose a directional flow for the
particles — forward or back."

"Back." He didn't really know what the particle
flow had to do with it or what to expect, so
it didn't make much difference.

"OK. Now turn the knob by your right thumb
to 157. Fine. Now the next one to it, turn that
to 'high'. There. Now push that little silver button
up above your head to 'on'. Good. Now ..."

Jeff felt a little queasy about the whole thing.
What if he made a mistake. But Uncle Zeke didn't
seem to think he could ruin anything so ...

"What are we going to see anyway?"

Just as he asked the question a grinding sound occurred. The computer flashed, "WAIT ... time acceleration in progress."

"It'll tell us when maximum speed has been reached and then ..."

Jeff felt himself spinning, twirling, pushed against the back of his seat as if a giant hand were flinging him around. He was feeling dizzy. This was worse than the rides he'd been on at the amusement park. Suddenly, a flash lashed out across the booth, shaking it violently. Jeff didn't see where it came from; his head was spinning wildly. Things were vibrating all around him and he couldn't hold himself onto the seat. He was conscious that his mother was screaming somewhere behind him. Everything seemed confused.

The air was gradually filling with greenish smoke. Was it smoke? Something like that. It made him cough and gasp for breath. Air. He must get air. He tried to scream. Tried to call his uncle. No sound came out. He was frozen, dumb. The whole cubicle was spinning violently now and it was hard to breath. Then he felt himself thrown backwards against the wall of the module. Hard. Everything was dark. He opened his eyes slowly, tentatively — blinked. Nothing. He could see nothing.

TWO

Where in the World am I?

Jeff rubbed the back of his head where it hurt. His fingers traced a marble-sized lump. Something warm trickled down his neck. He wiped it away and felt the stickiness on his fingers. It was blood. He must have cut his head when he fell. Or did he fall? What happened anyway?

Why couldn't he see anything?

A shrill voice hit his ears and, within seconds, other voices came closer and closer. He couldn't understand what they were saying but they seemed to have found him, wherever he was. Someone was touching him, carefully, almost gently.

"Hello," he said. "Hello. Who's here. I can't see. Where am I?"

The shrill voice said something. It seemed to be in answer to his question but he couldn't understand a word.

Gradually, a fuzzy light began to filter through his eyelids. Brighter and gradually brighter. The voices continued. Louder and more urgent-sounding by the minute. There must be a lot of people around him.

He could see light now, and gradually figures came into focus. It still seemed to be dark, maybe late afternoon on a cloudy day, but not as black as it had been. Now he could make out the people gathered around him. Everyone seemed to have black hair. He blinked and rubbed his eyes. This was weird. They were all Chinese. A Chinese man in a padded blue jacket was bending over him, helping him sit up. He raised himself on one elbow, cautiously, stiffly. He didn't seem to have any injuries other than the bump on his head.

"Where am I?"

The same insistent words came in answer. They were obviously trying to tell him something. Well, he didn't understand a word.

"Where am I anyway? Is this China? How did I get here? Oh, come on, somebody, speak English."

The faces looked friendly enough. At least the one bending over him did. It smiled. Jeff got to his feet now and sized up the situation. *If this is China, I must have traveled here in that experiment thing of Zeke's. But I thought that was supposed to be time travel. I must have traveled in time too. Forward or back? Back ... I remember choosing 'back'... What year is it anyway? I guess the experiment worked but ...*

Oh, man! have I done it! Here I am in ancient China and I'm stuck! Panic jolted through him like an electric shock. Then he calmed himself. *Uncle Zeke is at the controls. He knows what happened. He's going to push another button or two any minute and bring me back. It's kind of a joke, really. I'll probably only be here a minute or two so I'd better look around and take advantage of the adventure. Man, what a story I'll have to tell. Mom and Dad and Greg'll never believe this!*

The crowd seemed to be gathering more closely around him, jabbering all the while. It was, as he had thought, an overcast day with heavy clouds darkening the sky. He seemed to be in a town or city. The smell of the place made him gag. No more than ten feet from his head a couple of pigs and a scrawny dog nosed through the garbage a man had tossed onto the street. People scurried here and there around him, an ever-growing crowd. Hands were reaching out, touching him when they could get close enough. Someone touched his striped knit shirt and smiled. Someone else discovered the pockets in his jeans and seemed quite intrigued by them. One old lady with no front teeth was rubbing his light-colored hair between her fingers, an expression akin to awe on her face.

I've got to get out of here. Quit, quit, all of you, take your hands off me, Jeff thought. *If only the crowd would thin out I could make a break for it. Yuck, they're getting worse!*

"Hey, get out. That's my comb. Get your hands out of my pocket. Quit touching my face. Stop, stop. What is it with you guys?"

The answers continued to come from "shrill voice", the same as before, and just as unintelligible. He was smiling at Jeff, though, and seemed to be genuinely trying to be friendly.

Jeff forced himself to smile back. "Could you tell me how to get out of here?" *No, let me try that again. I've got to think of a word he might know. A city name.* "Peking," he said to the helpful one. "Peking. You know, your capital. Or is it? Anyway, it's the only big city I know." He tried again, forming the word very clearly and raising his volume to be heard above the rabble. "Peking. Pe-king. Where? How — do — I — go Peking? I," pointing to himself, "I ... go ... Peking." He pointed first one direction, then another. "Peking. That way? This way?"

It seemed to be amusing. But other than laughter and snickers from the fascinated crowd, he got no response.

Oh, hurry up, Uncle Zeke. Get me out of

here.

It was beginning to rain. *Oh, brother, just what I don't need.* Thunder and lightning pierced the air. Jeff stood still, trying to fend off the crowd a few minutes longer. The rain was pelting down. Another clap of thunder. More lightning. As if on cue the crowd began to disperse. As the rain increased, the crowd gradually thinned. One by one, people broke away from the attraction of a foreign boy, and headed for shelter. The rain was the best thing that could have happened. To think just a few hours ago he had been complaining about it.

Thunder and lightning now gripped the scene. Louder and closer the claps of thunder came. Everyone scattered, including "shrill voice", heading for stores and homes. Jeff realized he was quickly becoming soaked. But, what was more important, he was free from the crowd. Here was his chance. He looked around briefly. The road was narrow and filthy, winding its way between dark, stone buildings which seemed to be both house and store for the blue-gowned people scurrying into them.

He started to run along the cobblestone street, ducking under shelter as he went. But he realized he'd better not stay where he could be found so easily. When the rain stopped they would find him again. He must hide.

A tiny lane turned off to the right. No telling

where it went. He turned into it, wiping the rain out of his eyes as he ran so he could see one step ahead. What a storm! He'd never been in one this bad except the day the tornado almost touched down in their county. Tornados ... Did China have tornados? If so he sure didn't want to be in one. He stopped to rest under a building that overhung the street. Puddles formed at his feet and rain splashed and splattered on the cobblestones just in front of his nose, but at least here the rain wasn't pounding directly on him. He caught his breath. Where was Uncle Zeke? He should have figured out how to call him back by now!

Then a horrifying thought seized him. Maybe Uncle Zeke wasn't there. Maybe Uncle Zeke had been hurt too in whatever happened. Maybe no one knew where he was.

He fought down the sudden sick feeling that rose in his stomach. Rain continued to fall. It was becoming dark — must be about five or six o'clock, he guessed.

He looked out on a bleak scene, all greys and browns, sealed over with clouds. Off to the left stretched whole city blocks of nothing but rubble. Leftover bits of wall tottered here and there as ruined reminders of the city's past. If a giant bomb had dropped on the place it couldn't have looked more dilapidated.

There seemed to be no one living in the ruined

area, so Jeff headed that direction. He stopped in front of a curiously tilted shed with a few feet of roof left sagging in one corner. It appeared empty.

He picked his way across the ruins to the doorway and surveyed the hovel. Hay and mud matted the floor and there was no mistaking the lingering reek of past animal inhabitants. Rats scurried away as he approached. "Some place!" he said out loud, screwing up his nose as he entered. "But at least no one's here. I can probably escape attention for a while."

He chose the only spot sheltered by the remaining roof, stirred the hay to find some that was dry and sank down onto it, pulling his legs up into his body to keep warm. It took deliberate self discipline to ignore the spider hanging in its web no more than a foot away. He'd never been in such a filthy place.

He forced himself to size up the situation. The thought was beginning to gnaw at his mind that maybe Zeke wasn't going to bring him back after all. At least not for a while.

Slowly he began to digest the idea. He might not get home for a long time. Meanwhile he was cold, wet, alone, and couldn't communicate with anybody. Besides all that, his head was beginning to hurt. And by now it was night time so he couldn't hope to find his way out. He wished his Mom was there. Before he could stop

them tears rolled down his cheeks, mixing with
the rain that was already soaking his face. Who
cared? There was no one to see him, and anyway
he was too tired to resist. He would sleep, just
sleep. Then in the morning he must find help.
If morning ever came.

The mists of early morning hung feather-like over
the peaks in the distance. A pair of ducks glided
to a landing on the quiet waters of West Lake.
Within the city walls, a rooster crowed and a
couple of pigs started their day's foraging. The
sleeping city stirred and Jeff stirred also.

He was aware first of a headache, and a dull
pain in his right leg. Besides, he itched all over.
He sat up and began to scratch. Tiny red dots
covered his arms and legs and a miniscule black
speck hopped away as he touched it. Fleas! Even
without experiencing them before, he was sure
that's what they were.

The more he scratched, the itchier he felt. He
brushed a spider off his pant leg. Then suddenly
he remembered where he was, and the events
of the day before! Well, it was morning anyway.
At least he had lived that long. *Some hotel you
found*, he told himself. *As if the rats sharing
your mattress weren't enough, now you've got
fleas too.* If only he could get a hot shower.
Surely this was all just a nightmare; he'd go
downstairs and his Mom would pour him a glass

of orange juice like she always did and say, "Good morning, Jeff-boy. How about a bowl of cereal?" He got tired of hearing the same thing every day but boy, it sure would sound good about now. He brushed his hand through his tangled hair and felt again the bump on the back of his head. It still hurt, but the blood seemed to have dried.

Stepping out from under the sagging roof, he shivered. The air was cold and yesterday's rain left a lingering, penetrating dampness. He took a deep breath, rubbed some warmth into his arms, and began to inspect his surroundings more closely. He was in the midst of a patch of rubble, as if there had been a fire or something.

A few yards away the city wall rambled, thick and ageless, marking the edge of the city. How far it went, Jeff couldn't see. To his right stretched a long road that seemed to lead into the center of town. *Better than this junk heap anyway*, he thought. Of course, as soon as he headed towards town he would probably be mobbed again. But maybe he could also get something to eat. Wherever and whenever this was, it had to have food!

He headed down the road, away from the city wall towards the market area. Already it was awakening to a new day, though Jeff sensed that it was still very early. Chickens squawked and fluttered in front of an old peasant woman as she shuffled along a few hundred yards ahead of Jeff. He hoped she wouldn't turn around and see him.

On both sides of the road were once-palatial homes surrounded by walls, with large gardens and paths leading up to the door. Signs of past neglect were still evident, but obviously the houses had been restored somewhat and were being lived in again.

Now the street was getting busier as people appeared here and there to start the new day. Up ahead, one man was standing in front of his doorway, slowly moving through some kind of exercise routine, like aerobics in slow-motion.

Jeff's stomach was growling and he wished he knew how to ask for something to eat. Even a bowl of rice, if that's all they ate here, would be better than nothing. He wondered what his Mom and Dad and Greg were having for breakfast at his uncle and aunt's house. If it was morning there. It might not be. It might not even be this same month or year. Who knows. He had turned the flow of time backward, after all. Maybe he had really stepped back into yesterday. Oh, man, how did he ever get into this mess! If only he hadn't let Zeke talk him into trying out that experiment.

His mother and dad would be worried sick about him. He'd get something to eat, and then find a way out of here. Maybe get a ride to a bigger city, like Peking, where somebody would surely know what to do. There might even be a consul or ambassador there.

A man stopped sweeping the front of the store and looked at him curiously as he passed. Then he called something to a lady and a little boy, who came running out to see the sight. *I'm quite a curiosity piece, I see,* Jeff thought. As the city got more crowded, it was impossible to avoid being noticed. Word spread as he proceeded, and people came rushing from their stores to stare and giggle. Children ran out and followed a few feet behind him, talking and laughing but never quite daring to catch up. More children joined them, older brothers and sisters balancing babies on their hips, pointing out the fair-haired, white skin foreigner so younger ones too would learn to taunt such an oddity. Jeff wished a blanket would fall from the sky and cover him.

Safely behind the latest mob of children, a boy trailed. Taller than the others, less noisy in his ridicule, but nevertheless curious, he hung his head as if examining the road when Jeff turned around and saw him. But a few feet further on when Jeff rounded a corner, there he was again, perched on a cart, staring at him.

Jeff could smell something cooking. It seemed to be up ahead where a lady was squatting by a tiny black burner, fanning a reluctant flame to life. A metal wok perched on top of the fire and grease sizzled and sputtered. He was only a few steps from her as she dropped some batter into the pan, and the aroma reminded him of how hungry he was. Yesterday's breakfast was a long time ago! He smiled at the woman and considered asking her for one of the things she was cooking. But what would he say? More children had joined him, tagging along behind; adults watched suspiciously from doorways. The lady went on cooking without offering Jeff anything and he decided not to try to ask. He'd find some other way.

Three men stopped in front of Jeff and began talking. They seemed to be asking questions. One pulled at Jeff's teeshirt wonderingly. The other man poked at his chest, repeating something. *Oh, brother, here we go again,* Jeff thought. "No speak Chinese," he said loudly. They probably had no idea what he said, but it seemed best to say something.

The three were soon part of a small crowd that jostled and pushed. Jeff felt himself being propelled along toward the main business section of the street, where people were setting up stalls to sell food. Some of their wares looked familiar: oranges, bananas, and some green Chinese cabbage like his mum used for making chop suey. Next stall over a woman was laying out a newly killed chicken on the low wooden table that served as a counter. Blood was still running from its neck. The head was placed neatly beside the body, as if she expected to sell it too.

Grimacing, Jeff turned his head away. A couple of mangy curs fought over a scrap at his feet. He tried to push on, ignoring the gathering crowd. Increasing fear almost overcame his intense hunger.

A young man standing at the next market stall turned around as Jeff and his noisy entourage approached. He looked carefully at Jeff, and a cautious smile spread over his face as he walked purposely towards him. The tall boy had left his cart and was there again, standing by the sidelines waiting to see what would happen next.

Jeff didn't know what to do. He felt that any moment the smile could fade and a dagger could appear from under the loose blue padded gown. Was he friend or foe? There was no way Jeff could sidestep; the crowd surrounded him on all sides. He'd have to trust the young man — he didn't have much choice. He returned the smile, though fear crawled over him and he shivered a little.

The man nodded and bowed, all the while saying something.

"Hello," Jeff answered. After all, you've got to start somewhere.

"Hello," the young man answered.

Jeff couldn't believe his ears. English! But could he say more than that one word? Jeff responded excitedly, "Hello. Where am I? Can you help me?"

"Yes, yes. Come. Come." He motioned to Jeff to follow, beckoning him with an odd fingers-down motion.

"I'm very hungry. Can you give me something to eat?"

"Yes, yes. Come." Again, the same reply. *Maybe he can only say two words.* Hopeful now, Jeff tried again.

"Food. Do you have any food?"

"Yes, yes. Food. Come." He was nodding quickly as if he understood but couldn't say anymore. He seemed to be helpful though. Jeff was going to have to take the chance.

THREE
Over a hundred years ago!

Jeff followed the man through the increasingly busy street. The crowd seemed to make way for him and no one tried to touch him. He felt safer being with this Chinese guide. They passed a beggar sitting on a dirty piece of sacking by the roadside, his bony hands clutching a knobbly cane. His legs were stubs ending bluntly at calloused knees; his blind eyes flickered constantly, focusing on nothing. In a mournful sing-song, he cried and held out his hand to them as they passed. Jeff shivered and pulled himself in tightly, away from that skinny hand. He had nothing to give him anyway. He was glad the man couldn't see him.

As they neared the edge of the residential district, Jeff could see what was once a fountain, and some of the houses looked more like former palaces. Evidently it had been a high-class section, but something had changed all that. All around them was rubble, empty houses, old buildings half standing, burned or destroyed.

Jeff's self-made guide turned off the main street into a tiny lane. Near the corner where two whitewashed walls joined, an iron gate opened into a courtyard. A tiny sign attached to a post read, in English, "New Lane".

Jeff could see the area they were facing was big. It had probably been a mansion in its day, though now it looked more like a slum housing unit waiting for the wrecking ball. He followed his friend through the gate to a partially covered paved courtyard, with ten or twelve rooms around it. Through an open doorway in the west wall he could see a garden, and another wall beyond. It was obvious the place was being renewed and cared for, in spite of having fallen from its former glory.

Jeff's Chinese friend called out something and a man carrying a small can emerged from a doorway to the right, a man like Jeff had never seen before.

He was not Chinese. Of that Jeff was sure. He looked to be about thirty, a small man, blue eyed and fair skinned. Yet he had a Chinese-style braid of hair hanging down his back — probably would have been blond but dyed black, Jeff guessed — and was dressed, like the man

Jeff had followed, in a loose-fitting wadded blue gown with Chinese style black satin shoes. A black skull cap covered the front of his head where he had shaved off all his hair. Whoever he was, he was trying to look Chinese for some reason. Who was this guy anyway?

Jeff was soon put at ease when the "blond Chinese" held out his hand and introduced himself: "I'm Hudson Taylor. How can I help you?"

He had an English accent but the familiar language was music to Jeff's ears after what he'd just been through. His blue eyes twinkled with the smile that lit up his face as he looked over this strange visitor.

"Excuse me, I was just trying to see if I could improve the silver iodide mixture for my photographic plates." He glanced at the tin in his hand marked *Collodion*. "The plates dry out before I can get them exposed and fixed. Haven't had any successful photos since we arrived." He handed the tin to the Chinese man, who went into the house, and turned his attention to Jeff. "Now, you are?"

"I'm Jeff, Jeff Anderson. I don't know where I am and I'd like some help. I'd also like something to eat." He might as well tell them the truth.

Mr Taylor laughed and led Jeff across the courtyard. Jeff snuck a quick glance over his shoulder just in time to see the pock-marked face of his tall follower disappear behind the stone wall. He turned his concentration to where Taylor was taking him. They had entered a large room where several others were gathering for breakfast. The walls were bare, their gaping holes covered by a huge sheet of white paper. It was cold and wind whistled in where the paper didn't reach. Shelves built along one wall had ample room for the few tin plates, bowls and chopsticks they held. In the middle of the top shelf, conspicuous in contrast to the rest of the tableware, stood an English teapot. There was no furniture except two long trestle-like tables and benches, like rough picnic tables moved into a shed. *What goes here anyhow?* Jeff thought. *These people must be poor as dirt.*

"Maria," Mr Taylor called. "We've got a visitor. It seems he's a bit lost and Tsiu brought him to us. D'you think you can get the young man something to eat?"

A tired-looking young woman came into the room, with a toddler clinging to her long gown. The tiredness seemed to melt off her face when she smiled.

"Samuel, go and sit on your Papa's knee a minute while I get our friend a bowl and spoon." The little boy scurried over eagerly to Hudson Taylor who scooped him up in a big hug and kiss and planted him on one knee.

"When Papa finds a way to improve his photography I must take a picture of my boy. You're growing so quickly we must get a picture back to Grandmother in England."

Maria led Jeff to a place at the table nearest the door. She, too, was wearing Chinese clothes. But her smile was reassuring and the food the servant brought out for him was too good to leave. He'd eat first and ask questions later.

Maria seemed to understand this too as she waited patiently while he wolfed down the rice porridge and papaya they set out. A cup of hot Chinese tea washed it down and Jeff felt for the first time in two days as if maybe life would go on again after all.

"Now, tell us about yourself," Mr Taylor asked gently. "You say your name's Jeff. Jeffrey, I presume. Where are you from?"

"Yeah, Jeffrey, but I just go by Jeff. I'm from America. Minnesota actually. Not too far from Chicago — maybe you've heard of that."

"Yes, indeed. That's where that preacher is, that Mr D L Moody I've heard so much about. I'd like to meet him sometime. He's quite well-known in America, I believe. Perhaps you've heard of him."

Jeff gulped. Moody? The one who founded Moody Bible Institute? He'd lived a long time ago, surely! He nodded. "Yes, I've heard of him."

As he talked, Hudson Taylor flipped through a pile of papers someone handed him, putting his signature on some, adding a few words to others, deleting a line or two on another while still jiggling Samuel on one knee. And yet all the while Jeff felt as if Taylor was really listening to him, as though he focused his attention fully on Jeff without his long, agile fingers slowing down for a second.

Hudson laid his pen down for a moment, tickled Samuel's tummy, and said to Jeff, "Sorry I have to keep working while you're talking but I have 45 letters that must be sent today when the boat leaves. 45! Sometimes it's worse! As you'll soon see, I spend a lot of time writing. I think my pen will grow attached to my fingers any day now!" He set Samuel down and picked up his pen again. Jeff watched in silence as he continued working on the pile of paper.

"I was sorry to hear about the assassination of your President Lincoln," he was saying now. "Of course that was over a year ago,but I'm sure your country's still in shock over it. And has the situation settled down since the war between the States? Is everything back to normal again between north and south?"

Jeff stalled for an answer. "Uh, yes, I think so." He had to have some questions answered! "Where are we, and what year is it? I'm ... well, I'm a little confused."

"Goodness, yes, you must be. It's January, 1867. And this is Hangzhou, China. Are you all right? Did you get injured in some way?"

Jeff didn't know what to say. No wonder things seemed a bit out of date. It was over a hundred years ago! And how would he explain to Mr Taylor how he got here? He couldn't expect him to understand particle acceleration and time travel. He didn't understand it himself! They seemed to be waiting for an answer. What a strange sight he must be to them. Well, at least they were willing to help; he'd have to tell them something.

"I'm not supposed to be here. It's kind of an accident. I really can't explain it to you. I'm supposed to be in the United States, and I'm trying to get back there. But in the meantime if you could help me I'd appreciate it. I got into a crowd yesterday on the street and ... I think ... I think I've got a bump on my head."

They'll believe that easily enough, Jeff thought. *A bump on the head's putting it mildly!* They'd probably think he had a lot more than one bump to account for his appearance out of nowhere.

"Wait a minute! You say you're supposed to be in the United States. Then how on earth did you end up on the wrong side of the world? Were you on the wrong ship? Where are your parents? I've heard of strange things happening ... a ship goes off course or gets attacked by pirates ... heard of Chinese sailors rescuing a baby whose parents were killed in a shipwreck ... those things happen occasionally ... but, you say ..."

Maria put her hand on her husband's arm as if to calm his curiosity. She threw him a glance that Jeff interpreted as "Let me handle this," and turned to face Jeff. "Have you got parents, Jeffrey?" she asked quietly. "Are you an orphan? If you need a place to stay you're welcome to stay with us, but we'd like to know the truth."

Jeff swallowed and took a deep breath. He had to give some plausible explanation. "Yes, I have parents," he answered. "My Dad's a heart surgeon and my Mom's a librarian. I have a younger brother, too. Greg. They're back home in the United States.   We went to visit my uncle — he's a scientist — and he was experimenting with ... well, with spinning things around real fast, and I, ... I sort of got mixed up in one of his experimental machines. I don't know what happened, something exploded or something."

He paused. The Taylors looked like they were still waiting for the real story. Jeff straightened his shoulders and tried again. "Look, I can't explain it. I guess I blacked out or something. All I know is Uncle Zeke is probably doing all he can to fix the thing so he can get me back, so I won't be staying too long. But in the meantime ... please, just believe me. I really need your help."

Mr Taylor looked at Maria who patted Jeff on the arm comfortingly. He clasped and unclasped his long fingers as if working out his doubts. Jeff waited in silence.

Finally Hudson Taylor spoke. "Jeffrey, I can't understand what you're telling me. It is not possible for one to spin around fast, as you say, and catapult himself from America to China. Not possible. You must have embarked by ship; there's no other way to get here. Perhaps you've injured your head some way and you've forgotten who you are or where you came from. Perhaps you're making the whole thing up. I don't know. But I believe you that you have parents somewhere and you're lost. Obviously you need help. God has brought you here to us now for some purpose so I'm going to let you stay. But I will not put up with lying. As long as you're living with us you must tell the truth. Now, enough said. For now, I'll just overlook the discrepancies in your story and you may consider yourself part of the family."

Maria smiled and nodded. Obviously she agreed. "Wherever you came from, you do have a bump on your head. Hudson, can you attend to this for him?"

"Thank you," Jeff said. "Thanks a lot. I don't expect you to believe me or understand the story, but I really am telling the truth. If I can just stay with you for a few days until my uncle gets things fixed to bring me home, you'll see ... I won't lie to you. And I won't be any trouble either — just eat a bit," he added, grinning.

"Well, you're welcome to that." Maria laughed

and tied an apron around her waist. "We don't have much, but what God has provided for us we'll certainly share with you."

Nothing more was said about his mysterious appearance. Whatever Mr Taylor wondered, he joked and chatted casually as he led Jeff to another room across a small yard from the dining room. "This is my medical consulting room," Mr Taylor explained.

The door opened to a small room with cabinets along one wall, an examining table, a desk and, in the corner, a black iron pot perched on a glowing charcoal burner. Every inch of desk top was used: neat stacks of papers, pens, medical files arranged alphabetically in a wooden box, two well-thumbed textbooks, a microscope, a box of glass slides all labeled, and a half-inch stub of a candle. A diagram of the eye was nailed to one wall.

"I'm a doctor, you know. Trained in England. It's a blessing I did, too, I tell you. China has very little in the way of medical care out of the big coastal cities. Here, sit down and let me see your head." His long, thin fingers worked their way carefully, gently around Jeff's injury with no wasted motions.

While he treated, he talked. Jeff found out Hangzhou was an important city inland from Shanghai, on the Qiantang river and the Grand Canal.

"Marco Polo visited this city, you know, in the twelfth century. It has been a big, glorious city. Used to have a million and a half population. The imperial palace of the southern Song dynasty was here and they say it was exceptionally beautiful."

"What happened? It looks like a war zone or something."

"No wonder. You see, during the Taiping rebellion the city was besieged and burned three times. That accounts for the ruined areas on the outskirts. In fact we only got this big house for a reasonable price because it is surrounded by acres of ruins. But we're fixing it up. You should have seen it a month ago!" He laughed. A hearty laugh, Jeff thought, considering the dump he lived in.

"What are you doing here? How come all of you live like this and — well, wear these clothes and all?"

"You're not the first to wonder that, my boy. We're from England, and we're missionaries, all of us. Christian missionaries. Not the first, mind you, but the others all live on the coast — Shanghai, mostly — among other westerners like themselves. When I first came to China and saw how many people there were in the interior, with hardly any missionaries at all among them, I knew that's where I had to go."

He pulled out another roll of clean white sheeting

which he quickly tore into strips. Then he continued, "Maria and I were ready to move inland and just trust God to provide for us, but we didn't know if anyone else would be willing to join us. After all, I couldn't promise them a penny. But ... we prayed and one by one others who had the same goals teamed up with us — all the people you see here and more to come. And God sends the money necessary to provide for them."

Jeff nodded. His church had missionary speakers from time to time. They all talked about God providing for them. In fact, come to think of it, he may even have heard the name Hudson Taylor. He never pictured him looking like this, though. "What about the clothes?"

"Oh, yes, the clothes. Well, we dress like the Chinese because they're much more willing to listen to what we have to say when they see we identify with them — wear their clothes, eat their food and so on. Here, turn your head this way so I can see what I'm doing." Taylor twisted a bandage deftly around Jeff's ear.

"In fact, we've found it a great help so far. We can go out on the streets with much more safety like this — I know because I have tried it both ways."

"Yeah, I know what you mean. I was surrounded in no time out on the street and they poked and pulled till I thought I'd be torn in two. I guess Chinese clothes would be safer."

"Not everyone agrees, mind you," Hudson Taylor went on. "Some of the government people and missionaries from other societies — even, I'm afraid, some in our own mission. They can't understand why we've adopted this 'crazy idea', as they think. But time will prove it wise, I'm convinced."

"Who was the man who led me here?"

"Tsiu Kyuo-kwe. He's a Christian helper. Doesn't know much English, as you probably found out, but he's a good preacher."

Mr Taylor was finished now and Jeff felt gingerly at the bandage tied around his head. It wasn't the way his doctor in Minnesota would have done it, he was sure, but it did feel better. Hudson Taylor went on to put ointment on all the bug bites from the night before. As he worked he talked. And Jeff asked more questions.

"How long have you been here?"

"Oh, I came out to China originally by myself a long time ago, but we — our group here — came out from England on the ship *Lammermuir*, just last May."

As they left the clinic they passed a group of Chinese sitting in the courtyard and the adjoining waiting room. "More patients," Taylor said, nodding toward them. "Looks as if I'd better get to work. You are welcome to stay as long as you need to. Go and see my wife, Maria, or Miss Faulding if you have any needs."

If I have any needs, Jeff thought. *Boy, do*

I have needs! I need to figure out what's going on. I need to get out of here. I need to go home ... He stepped out into the courtyard again. Maria was passing by and stopped to introduce him to the rest of the household.

"This is Miss Emily Blatchley. She helps me look after the children, and is Hudson's secretary too. Such a help, she is." Emily smiled shyly and attempted to wave off the compliments. She was slim and neat, dark hair piled on her head in Chinese style. She was carrying an armful of letters and books to Mr Taylor's office. "Oh, yes, you are, Emily. The most efficient person I've ever seen — except for my husband, of course." Maria smiled and gave Emily a quick hug. Apparently they were good friends.

"And Miss Jenny Faulding," Maria continued, introducing a rosy-cheeked young lady with a smile that seemed to be constantly threatening to become a laugh. Jeff had to smile in return. "You'll soon see how much she does. We hadn't been here a month when Jenny had women meeting regularly to study the Bible. Most of the Christians you'll see meeting now in our little church on Sunday are contacts Jenny made one way or another." She flashed a warm smile at Jenny who was buttoning another jacket over her clothes.

Jenny grinned and held out a hand to Jeff. "Pleased to meet you. I'll have to talk to you later. I'm going to visit Miss Wang if I can find her house. And then I'll stop by the shipping office to see if any new mail has come in for us. As if Mr Taylor needs any more letters to answer!"

"Thank you, Jenny. And this is George Duncan, and Mr Rudland ..."

The names were running into a blur in Jeff's mind. He couldn't remember them all, but everyone seemed friendly. And happy, which was the queer thing, when you saw how they lived. Kind of normal people, but certainly not a normal way to live. He could probably get to like them well enough in time ... though of course he wouldn't be staying that long.

Just then a little boy came running down the stairs and into the courtyard, grabbing Maria's skirt.

"This is my son, Herbert," Maria said, beaming at the boy. "Herbert, shake hands with our guest."

The little boy reached out one hand and shook Jeff's vigorously.

"Hello. I'm Herbert Hudson Taylor. They call me Bertie," he announced. "You can too. I'm six."

Not shy anyway, Jeff noticed. *Smart kid. Kind of cute. Except for that English accent, he's sort of like Zeke and Nonie's little boy, Andy.*

Bertie continued to pour out information, chattering on happily. "We've only just settled in here. We came on a big ship from London. Do you know what the ship was called? *The Lammermuir*. Isn't that a funny name? It was very bumpy. We had such bad storms we thought we'd all be washed overboard."

Jeff felt himself relax as he listened.

"But Papa prayed and God made the storm calm down. After we got here we had no place to live. We had to stay squashed up in the tiny rooms on the ship. There was no room to throw my ball around. We didn't even know anyone who could help us. But then God gave us this great big house. Do you like this big house? Mama and Papa are going to fix it up better. It's got so much room. Freddie and I can have our own room and lots of place to play. Do you want to see our nice room? You can sleep in our room, too."

All that seemed to be said without stopping for breath. Jeff grinned at him. *At least I won't be lacking for conversation,* he thought to himself.

"Who's Freddie?"

"My brother. He's five. Then there's Samuel, who's three. And there's Gracie, over there. The one with the plate in her hand. She's eight. We're all very sociable and intelligent children. Papa says so. You'll see."

Jeff laughed. "If the others are half as intelligent and sociable as you are, Bert, that'll be enough! Do you ever stop talking?"

"Herbert, hush now," Gracie called to him. "Time to get to our studies. Go and get your books."

She smiled at Jeff as she passed, a shy, pretty smile. Like everyone else in the house, she was wearing Chinese-style clothes — a long tunic with a stand-up collar over baggy satin pants and black felt shoes. Across the top of her head ran a ribbon which ended in a tuft of flowers at each side, just above her temples. Just like a picture of a Chinese child in a history book. And yet, so English. It would be easy to imagine her in a parlor in England.

"Glad to meet you, Jeff." She curtsied slightly and added, "Now if you'll excuse us, please, Miss Emily says we must get to our lessons. Mama doesn't like us to be late."

Jeff was speechless. This was unbelievable. He struggled to take in everything that was going on. Here were these people, even kids, living in this poor house, freezing cold, wearing that awkward, funny-looking Chinese outfit, but happy, or they seemed so anyway, and so polite. And even keeping up with their schooling! Somehow that made sense; he could easily believe that Maria and Emily would make them be prompt and regular in their studies. It just seemed to go with everything else he was observing. No excuses. No complaining. Just doing what had to be done. Incredible! These people were something else!

He felt a little ashamed of himself for complaining about yesterday's rain and all. At least he had a roof over his head now, and people who spoke English.

Tsiu was motioning for him to come with him. He followed his Chinese friend upstairs.

"Master Taylor bedroom," Tsiu said, pointing to a small room off to the right. On the wall opposite the door Jeff noticed a big painting of a young man with blond curly hair, dressed in an old-fashioned black suit coat, shirt with pointed collars standing up under the chin, wide bow tie, the picture of an English gentleman.

"Is Mr Taylor," Tsiu said, beaming. "Honorable aunt paint face."

Jeff puzzled momentarily. "His aunt, Mr Taylor's aunt, painted the picture? Is that what you mean? It's a portrait of him?"

"Yes, yes." Jeff could see the resemblance now, although shaving off his hair in front and dyeing the remainder black, and wearing Chinese garb, sure had changed the man's looks.

Jeff stuck his head around the door curiously. Over the low wooden bed that filled one corner of the room was a pink and white flowered bedspread. Must have been something they brought from England. A brightly painted wooden box served as storage chest and seat. On top of it two embroidered pillows leaned against the wall. In the far corner, on a tripod, stood an antiquated camera. That was what Mr Taylor was making the plates for, Jeff guessed. All that just to get a photo! A glass frame on the wall displayed a dozen butterflies, mounted and labeled. The floor had a woven bamboo mat. Though still very sparse and barren, there was an air of hominess about this room that the rest of the house lacked. Something about the personality of the Taylors. Up here in their own private room it seemed they showed another side of their lives.

Tsiu leaned a little closer now and lowered his voice as if letting Jeff in on secrets only he had acquired. "Come from great honorable family, Mr Taylor. Live nice, much culture. Very wise man, Mr Taylor."

Jeff nodded.

"How did you get to know them?" he asked Tsiu who seemed happy to show off his connection with the Taylors.

"Long time ago. Humble Tsiu live in Ningbo. Mr Taylor come to tell Jesus way. Tsiu believe and read God's Book. Teach honorable mother to read also. Now mother believe too."

"Your mother? She's a Christian too, is that what you mean?"

"Yes, yes. By read God's Book. When Mr Taylor come back to China Tsiu come from Ningbo to help."

Tsiu suddenly remembered the errand that had brought them upstairs. He beckoned with his fingers down, like Jeff had noticed him doing before, and scurried to the next doorway. "Come, come. Follow please."

Right next to the Taylor's was the room Jeff was to share with Bertie and Freddie. Tsiu pointed to a narrow wooden bed along one wall, covered with straw, over which was a thin felt mattress. A patchwork quilt, obviously brought out from England, covered that and relieved the drabness. At the head was a pillow of sorts — a fat cylinder about eighteen inches in diameter and hard as a rock. Jeff thanked Tsiu who smiled, bowed and disappeared downstairs.

A great feeling of homesickness washed over him and the greens and purples of the quilt patches blurred before his eyes as he buried his face in them and sobbed.

FOUR
Life in Hangzhou

Jeff woke up shivering. Wind whistled through the gaping holes in the wall. Last night's embers that still glowed in the small charcoal burner were helpless against the February cold.

That was one advantage of his Chinese clothes. An old jacket of Mr Taylor's had been shortened and taken in by Maria to fit him. He had felt funny in it at first, and even now he wore his own teeshirt at bedtime, but he had to admit one thing — the Chinese jackets were warm.

He piled the quilt higher around Bertie and Freddie who were still asleep in the double bed they shared. Bertie stirred; his breath hung in visible puffs on the frigid air. He would be awake in a minute or two, but for now Jeff eased himself carefully from his side of the bed and pulled on his black baggy pants and blue gown in a race against the goose bumps that popped out all over his bare back.

He was fitting into the routine by now. The days began early. By the time dawn outlined the pagoda on the hill Mr Taylor was already busy. Jeff usually got up then too: it was too cold to sleep late anyway. It seemed like a far distant dream that he had once been able to sleep till ten o'clock in a bed where your breath didn't freeze over on the edge of the sheet. That was luxury, like hot showers and microwave pizza! He never thought he'd miss silly little things like that so much.

And it wasn't just that. All these people jabbering around him in Chinese day and night, people staring at them through the gate, everybody parading around in these stupid oriental clothes with black pigtails hanging down their backs as if they were Chinese. And prayers, every day at noon for a whole hour. Prayers and Bible reading — the whole household had to be there. Yesterday he had gotten restless and started rolling and unrolling a thread on his jacket. Miss Blatchley had looked at him very sweetly and reached over to tap his hand. How much more of this could he stand? If Uncle Zeke didn't get things fixed and bring him home soon he'd go crazy!

There wasn't one luxury that he could find in this whole dilapidated house. Not one thing he could really enjoy about living here. He pulled a shoe on vigorously. Not that anyone else was miserable. As a matter of fact they all seemed content. "Content with whatever our heavenly Father sends." That was how Mr Taylor put it. Well, he had to admire their attitude, even though he couldn't live this way.

Bertie's voice, still half asleep, made him turn. "Are you going to help Papa again today?"

"Oh, hi. You're awake now, are you? Yeah, I guess so. I try to help him in the clinic in the mornings 'cause that's when he's the busiest. But after that I have to help Mr Rudland ink the printing press."

"Well, when you finish will you help us?"

"Help you what?"

"Help us clear the rocks from the ground behind the kitchen so as soon as the weather warms up we can plant a garden."

"I can't believe it's ever going to get that warm, but sure, I'll help you when I finish my other jobs."

"We have to move the goats today, too. They've eaten all the grass in that corner."

"Okay, I'll give you a hand if I have time. We have to check on your father's horse, too. He said it seemed to be limping yesterday."

It was good to have something to do so he didn't feel like a dead weight on the household. And as long as he was busy he didn't have time to think about being homesick.

As a matter of fact, this was the busiest household he'd ever seen. Mr Taylor himself had enough work for ten men. He had all the responsibilities of the leader — writing reports, settling disputes, orientating new workers, negotiating with the government — besides evangelizing new towns, translating the Bible into the language spoken by the local people, writing articles to inform people in England about his work and, of course, carrying on the clinic and preaching. Besides that, he still squeezed in time occasionally for his photography or to play hymns on a little foot-powered organ. Jeff was glad to help in any way he could. It wasn't the work he minded; it was the constant crowds that bugged him.

He hadn't finished dressing when he heard the *creeeak* that meant Tsiu was opening the gate to let in the early students. Why did they always have to start arriving before he could even eat breakfast? Didn't they have any idea of time?

"There's Mama's first student," Bertie said, dangling his feet over the edge of his bed.

"Uh-huh. Your mother doesn't seem to mind how early they get here."

"Of course not. She wants them to come."

Maria had started a school for women. While they learned to sew, she read the Bible to them and explained the gospel. Then, for an hour before they went home, Jenny would teach them to read. By now several could read simple parts of the Bible for themselves.

"Yeah, I know. It's just ... well," Jeff shrugged,

"... it gets kind of crowded around here sometimes, that's all."

He did up the last button on his high-necked jacket, ran a comb through his hair and headed downstairs. Maybe he could get to the dining room before too many more people arrived. Once the patients started pouring into the clinic there would be no privacy for the rest of the day.

He slid into a spot at the end of the long wooden table and picked up a spoon. Rice filled you up but it sure was tiresome when you had it for breakfast, dinner and supper. Well, what was this? Today there was some kind of melon or other to go with the rice. He reached for a piece with his fingers, feeling Emily's disapproving eyes on him. He knew he should have used his chopsticks but fingers were easier. What he wouldn't give for a couple slices of crinkly bacon and a fried egg. Boy, if his Mom could see him now! She would never believe he'd actually eat Chinese green vegetable and bean sprouts. Even the slimy grey "cheesey" stuff called "tofu". He'd never be caught dead eating it at home. Not even in tofu ice cream. But when you got hungry enough and that was all there was ... He'd nearly gagged on it the first time or two, but now he could put it in his mouth, chew it and have it slip down quickly without letting himself think about it. Besides it really wasn't too bad, cooked the way they did it here; and, George Duncan kept assuring him, "It'll make you bonny."

Jeff was learning to appreciate the big Scottish stonemason, whom everyone seemed to call simply "Duncan". Besides a sense of humor that often made his sandy eyebrows twitch with glee, he had a quiet strength about him Jeff admired. It was easy to feel comfortable around George Duncan.

He shoved away another bowl of rice when Duncan offered it. "No, thanks. I'm up to here in rice," he said, running his hand across his forehead. "What're you goin' to do today, Duncan? Drink tea all day as usual?"

Duncan laughed. "I'll get waterlogged with all my tea-drinking, for sure. But, I tell you, Jeffrey, that's the best way to learn the Chinese language, at least the dialect they speak here. Just sitting in the tea-houses with the other men and listening to them hour after hour."

"I s'pose so. Seems kind of like a waste of time. But I guess you're right about it being a good way to learn Chinese. How's it coming anyway?"

"Very slowly. In fact, I'm fearing it'll take my dull brain longer than anyone else's. Sometimes I wonder if I'll ever be able to preach in it."

"Oh, I've listened to you practice and I'd say you're as good as anyone else. I heard Jenny saying she's still learning and she's been here longer than you have. Mr Rudland's having a hard time too, I think. So you're not alone. Besides, you can understand a lot already. It won't take long till you're as good as Mr Taylor."

"Aach, I wish it were so. But I'll keep at it. I've got to be able to get along on my own so I can leave Hangzhou and open a new station in the interior."

"Where?"

"I don't know yet. But there's so much territory out there with no missionaries, no Christians ... eleven huge provinces with no one. I didn't leave Scotland to sit in a city with other missionaries. I've got to reach out to a new place. I'd like to be out on my own before the year's up."

"You will." He had often listened to Duncan as he practiced the rising and falling tones and rolled his Gaelic tongue around the strange syllables. No doubt about it, he had perseverance. "You'll soon be sounding so much like a Chinese they won't know the difference."

Duncan laughed. "If you can have a Chinese with a Highland brogue, maybe. One good thing about sitting in the teahouses all day, Jeffrey, is that I hear what's going on, hear what people are thinking."

"What's that?"

"Oh, nothing specific but I sense a certain un-easiness ... dissatisfaction maybe. I don't think for-eigners have been accepted very well in some cit-ies."

"Hmmm. Yeah, they weren't too friendly to me when I first arrived either. At least until I put on Chinese clothes. But they seem to like us well enough now. Or at least they like Mr Taylor's free clinic. From the sounds of it, there's a crowd already waiting. I gotta go."

He shivered as he walked across the courtyard to the chapel. Brr. Would this place ever get warm?

Since the chapel adjoined the clinic, it was used as a waiting room and this morning Jeff counted 73 patients already. By the end of the day, he figured there'd be at least 125, like yesterday. Seemed like more every day. Tsiu was already at work sorting through some large posters. He smiled at Jeff and showed him the pictures. "I look one to tell."

"To tell about?" Jeff answered. "Oh, I see, you're going to use one as an illustration and preach from it. Okay, you should say, 'I'm finding one to preach about'."

"I'm finding one to preach about," Tsiu repeated good-naturedly. He and Jeff had an understanding; in exchange for his help to Jeff in many ways, Jeff would help him improve his English. They both benefitted and Jeff was glad Tsiu was now learning enough to be able to talk to him. In fact Jeff was learning some Chinese too. Yesterday Tsiu had spent nearly an hour teaching him how to count.

"I've got to help in the clinic. See you later." He went on into the little treatment room, rubbing his hands together for warmth. He hated these cold early mornings. His fingers were so cold he could hardly lay out the instruments Mr Taylor needed.

"Probably be a few cataracts ... let me have both my eye surgery kits," Taylor instructed.

"You're getting pretty popular for your eye surgery," Jeff said. "That lady that you did last week, for instance, she was so excited she says she's going to send her sister. And yesterday you had — how many, three more?"

"Yes. It's a simple enough procedure really, but to them it's a miracle. To see when you've been blind ... there's nothing quite as dramatic. I can see why they'd be excited."

"Sure. But you aren't going to have time to eat or sleep if it goes on like this. More every day. And you've still got that cough." He wanted to add, "and no wonder, living in this icebox."

"Now you're sounding like Maria," Taylor said, laughing. "I do need help, that's true. Dr McCarthy is on his way out from England to help. I'll be glad when he comes. Meanwhile, the Lord will give strength."

Jeff said nothing. He had heard that kind of reply before. It was typical of Mr Taylor to just expect God to look after things. Well, help better come soon. Mr and Mrs Taylor couldn't keep this up forever.

Jenny Faulding stuck her head around the corner to ask about an errand Taylor wanted done. "I can do it on my way over to the palace. I've been invited there for tea this morning," she said, smiling. Her nose was red with the cold; she stepped over beside Jeff and touched her icy fingers to the back of his neck, laughing as he jumped and hollered. Hudson Taylor turned to see what was going on and joined in the laughter, eyes twinkling, as he cheered Jenny on.

"That's it! That's it! Wake the boy up!"

"All summer my hands were so itchy with insect bites I could hardly stand it," said Jenny, "and this time of year they're so cold they're like blocks of ice. I'm glad at least I don't have to walk across town in this cold, or my fingers would be frozen completely. In fact, my transportation is waiting at the gate now," she said, waving as she went out the door.

"That lady has more invitations than all of us put together," Taylor said when she had gone. "Almost every day she's invited to the home of some high-ranking lady. Wives of dignitaries, mind you. They send their own sedan chairs for her — that shows how they respect her."

"I guess that'd be like sending ..." he stopped himself just in time from saying, "your private limousine and chauffeur for a VIP," and changed it to "your coach and livery for an aristocrat."

"Yes. And, it's not only the upper class ladies that want to see her, but everyone; everywhere she goes she's welcomed. We could do with more of her kind."

"I can see why people like her; she's nice."

"The Chinese call her 'Miss Happiness'. Appropriate, isn't it?"

"That's for sure. Miss Happiness and Miss Energy."

After a while, Jeff left the treatment room and moved into the clinic. The charcoal burners had taken the chill off the air somewhat, and the crowd of patients seemed to hardly notice the temperature as they sat listening. A partition down the middle divided the audience, according to Chinese custom, men on one side and women on the other. At the front stood Tsiu, pointing to a large poster showing a heart with lots of different kinds of animals in it.

Bertie had explained it all to Jeff a few days before. Something about the pig standing for gluttony, the peacock for pride and so on. By now Tsiu was probably telling the audience how all these evil things in the human heart could be forgiven by trusting the Lord Jesus as Savior.

The reactions were mixed. Some of the old people didn't seem to understand a word. One man sat moaning and rubbing his arm, which was covered with open sores. Beside him a boy coughed violently and spat on the floor. A younger man sat cross-legged, balancing a badly deformed child stiffly on his lap.

Over on the other side a woman nursed her baby, coughing all the while. Older women with leathered faces and black teeth talked among themselves. A young girl about twelve years old stood at the back juggling a baby on one hip, a metal bowl in her hand. As Jeff watched she dipped her fingers into the dish, scooped up something and stuffed fingers and all into the baby's mouth, temporarily stifling his cries. A few children whined. The baby on the girl's hip yelled again.

But here and there throughout the crowd, Jeff noticed, some were really listening. In fact, he recognized the man on the front row. He had been here every day this week and he had nothing wrong with him. It seemed he came just to hear the teaching.

After a few minutes Tsiu changed to a poster showing a big canyon with a cross stretching across it. It was supposed to represent the big gap between God and men because of sin, and the cross as the only way to bridge that gap. When Tsiu began to get tired, Mr Taylor himself came out of the clinic for a while and took his turn preaching. It was like this every day. The medicine and the message seemed to go together, and both were welcomed, at least by some.

Already in the months the missionaries had been here three or four had prayed to receive Jesus Christ as Savior. Now they came every day just to hear more. You could tell by their eyes they liked what they heard.

It's hard to believe people have really never heard all this before, Jeff thought as he watched. It was the same stuff he'd heard in Sunday School and church since he was a baby. He was almost bored with it. Here was a grown man eating up every word like it was wonderful news.

"I know the word 'gospel' means 'good news'," he told Duncan later, "but I've never thought of it that way before. Like something you've waited for all your life, and finally someone tells you it's actually happened. These people really get excited when they hear it."

As the crowd gradually received treatment and left for home, Jeff noticed a boy lingering by the door. It was the boy who had watched him so curiously when he arrived. *What's he after anyway?* Jeff wondered. He might have been there during Tsiu's message, but he had not been in to see Mr Taylor for treatment; he seemed to be just looking. He ran out as Jeff entered the chapel, but once safely outside the gate he stayed, peering in the fence, staring at all that was going on. He looked to be about Jeff's own age. His head seemed almost too big for his thin body. A shock of black, wiry hair flopped down over his forehead accenting his face with its badly marked complexion. One eye seemed to have something wrong with it. Was he cross-eyed? Injured maybe? Jeff didn't know, but he felt funny having the boy staring at him like that.

He strode over to the gate and waved his arms in an angry shooing motion. The drivers of sedan-chairs, parked hopefully outside the gate, noticed his anger and laughed, making comments Jeff couldn't understand. He felt his face get hot. The boy didn't move. Jeff glared at him fiercely, delivering a silent message, then turned his back and walked deliberately away.

Suddenly Jeff was aware that there seemed to be a lot of running around. He went out into the courtyard to see what was going on. A servant girl appeared at the door of the clinic and called Mr Taylor, who ran across the courtyard before Jeff could ask him what was happening. Miss Faulding hurried from the kitchen with a basin of hot water. Chinese servants came in and out of rooms, scurrying and shuffling with more urgency than usual. A few minutes later Herbert came running down the stairs and grabbed Jeff's hand.

"We have a new baby! We have a new baby! A sister! Isn't that nice? Come and see!" He pulled Jeff towards the stairs.

So that was it! He hadn't ever expected to find himself right in the house where a baby was being born! Wow! Right here this very morning and he didn't even know about it! Why, Maria had been working in the kitchen just an hour ago. "Good thing your father's a doctor," he said to the bouncing figure beside him. That was something he had always taken for granted — that there would be a doctor somewhere in town when you needed one. It shocked him to realize they had no medical help around except Mr Taylor himself and what he could do with the primitive instruments in that treatment room.

Bertie led him into the Taylors' room where Miss Blatchley and Miss Faulding and all the Taylor children were gathered around the bed, looking at a tiny lump in a big blanket. Emily held Samuel in her arms so he could see better. Hudson Taylor was standing to one side, relieved and proud. Maria lay beside the wrapped bundle, smiling, and seeing that everyone got his turn to touch the infant. Jeff rubbed his finger gently on the tiny face that peeked out, red and wrinkled, eyes closed, from above the sheet. "She's pretty cute," he said softly. "What are you going to call her?"

Hudson answered quickly, "This one's after you, my dear. We'll call her Maria."

Maria added wearily, "For both of us. Her name will be Maria Hudson."

"Maria Hudson Taylor, born February 3, 1867." It had a good sound to it.

Jeff found himself gradually becoming involved in the lives of these people who had befriended him. He couldn't resist Herbert, and Gracie's quiet smile won him every time. And, although he sure wouldn't choose to live this way, he had to admire Mr Taylor. No matter what happened that man stayed calm and cool. He never seemed to get angry with his kids or the other missionaries, or even the servants who were pretty stupid sometimes. And he worked like he was made of iron or something — never got tired. Well, never let it slow him down anyway. He seemed to relax by playing the funny little organ and singing, by walking out into the hills and catching butterflies or bugs and recording them, or by working on his photography. Jeff got frustrated just watching him try to keep the silver-covered plates wet while he took a picture and rushed to develop it. *What would he think of my polaroid camera if he could see it?* he wondered.

And Maria, how could you *not* like Maria? Tall, graceful, quiet Maria. She had a sense of humor that always brightened the day — even when Mr Taylor seemed most worried about something, she could coax a laugh out of him. Whatever his objections about being here, Jeff was beginning to feel like part of the family. He was even beginning to understand a few Chinese words.

But that didn't mean he wanted to stay. He had searched his brain for any possible idea that would get him home again, but none came to mind — none that would work, that is. There was just no way. He had even thought of taking a boat from Shanghai, if Taylors would help him get there, but that would only land him in the United States of the 19th Century. That wasn't much better — it still wasn't home. And besides, it would take months, and in the meantime he might miss Uncle Zeke who was probably trying to contact him even now. He threw down the book he was reading in frustration. No matter how desperate he was there was nothing he could do about it. Zeke would be working on it, no question of that. He could only wait.

"If you thought there were a lot of patients waiting yesterday, you should see it now!" Duncan said one morning as he came into the dining room where Jeff was helping Miss Blatchley put out round cakes with thin red glaze on top. They were special for Chinese New Year.

"Yeah, they seem to use their holiday to come to the doctor. Not much of a holiday, if you ask me."

"Oh, Chinese New Year is probably the only day off most of them will have all year long. It's their only chance to be treated for whatever ails them. Good opportunity for us too. Think of all these people who can hear the gospel at one time."

"Mr Taylor will take advantage of it, you may be sure," Miss Blatchley said, nodding.

"How come it's New Year's in February?" Jeff asked as he licked his finger and made a face at the taste.

"Goes by the moon," Duncan answered. "Changes every year, not like our set calendar in the West. It's usually some time in February but not always the same date."

"Do they do anything special? Special food or something?"

Duncan picked up one of the round cakes and devoured it in two bites. "Eat these, for one thing. And look at the crowd out there, you'll see most of them have new clothes. They try to buy a new outfit for the occasion. Especially for the children. And they visit each other — rather like Christmas caroling at home but with no carols." He laughed heartily. "No plum pudding either, sad to say."

Jeff grinned back. "You can have your plum pudding. I'll take pie, apple pie, pumpkin pie, any pie."

Just then Mr Taylor came into the room and began dragging out a sturdy-looking table. "Give me a hand with this, will you, please?"

Jeff ran over and grabbed one end. They pulled it into the courtyard where the crowd was already overflowing from the chapel-cum-waiting room. More heads were peeking in from the lane through the gateway. *Probably two or three hundred at least,* Jeff thought to himself. They were a happier crowd today than usual, laughing and talking and pushing in for a look at the "white man". Sure enough, most of them did have something new on.

"It's Chinese New Year," Bertie announced, appearing alongside them. "D'you know what?"

Jeff had learned that Bertie didn't need an answer to continue. "At New Year's everyone gives little gifts of money to children and cook's going to give us some too."

"Not a bad custom," Jeff laughed. "I wouldn't mind them doing that back home. Is that what's in those red envelopes? Money?"

"Yes. They all come to visit, too, and Papa says it's a good time to get lots of people to listen to the gospel."

Hudson Taylor was lifting his small organ up to the table now. "Oh, good, Papa's going to play the harmonium," Bertie shouted, clapping his hands.

"Is that what you call that thing? It looks like a little organ to me. Only handier, because you can cart it around with you."

Hudson Taylor jumped up on the table and began to sing and play, pedaling the little instrument vigorously. His fingers, as always, moved skillfully and easily over the keys. Under his hands, it sounded almost as good as a pipe organ in a cathedral. "Man, think what he could do with a synthesizer," Jeff said to Bertie, then realized it was a good thing Bertie hadn't heard him because that would take a lot of explaining.

The crowd gradually grew quiet. Jeff watched, fascinated, as Mr Taylor went on, singing one piece after another, while the crowd stood speechless, with none of the usual coughing or shuffling. They were apparently enjoying the entertainment. And Mr Taylor was enjoying himself every bit as much.

"Your father actually knows every verse of all those hymns by memory! What a lot of work."

"Oh he didn't memorize them, he wrote them. Or some of them he translated into Chinese from English. Mama helped him."

Then Mr Taylor stood up and began to speak. Jeff had no idea what he was saying but it must have been something the crowd wanted to hear because the attention continued.

The crowd at the gate was moving now, making way for someone. Jeff saw a man and lady with four small children push their way into the courtyard. They were English, Jeff guessed, though they, too, were wearing Chinese dress. They seemed to be expected; Tsiu ran over to greet them.

They stopped and turned their eyes to where Mr Taylor was still standing on the table, preaching lustily to the attentive crowd. After a minute, he spotted the newcomers and his face broke into a grin. "Hello, John and Margaret. Welcome to Hangzhou." They waved at him and moved on into the house.

Without a second's hesitation Mr Taylor went right back to preaching. Jeff left the crowd and followed the newcomers into the dining room. "Are you the new doctor that's come to help? Mr Taylor's been expecting you." He shook hands with them both, offered them some tea, and found a newly baked cookie for each of the children.

John McCarthy smiled and turned to his wife. "Well, Margaret, I'm satisfied. We came to help a busy man and it looks like we're certainly going to be needed."

FIVE
Helping Out

With Dr McCarthy there, the medical work got easier. At least now there was someone capable of mixing the drugs Hudson Taylor prescribed and giving them to the Chinese helper with instructions for the patient. Jeff still helped out in the clinic every day and often, as he walked across the courtyard to the clinic, he saw his thin-faced observer at the gate, watching silently in the shadows. Yelling at him did no good. Jeff wished he could pull down a sky-to-ground curtain that would hide their whole compound from view. He hated being stared at. He glared back at the boy.

He couldn't worry about him for long, though; there was too much to do.

"I thought I'd be bored to death," he said to Gracie Taylor one day. "I'm used to a big city with lots of things going on. School, church, youth group, junior choir, basketball, band practice, things to do on weekends. Always something. And even when I'm not out there's stuff to do at home ..." He was going to say "like TV", but stopped himself. "I thought there'd be nothing to do here at all, but I'm so busy I hardly have time to think." In fact that was the one thing he didn't have time for — thinking of a way to get back home. Every night as he lay awake in the dark he tried to concentrate on coming up with a plan. But by then he was so tired he'd fall asleep. Now he didn't think about it as much as he used to.

He patted the nose of the small horse Taylors kept in the neighboring field. Later on this afternoon, if there was time, he might go for a ride. Mr Taylor had bought the horse for fun and exercise — it seemed he had been a good horseman in England. But he let Jeff borrow it as often as he wanted to. Sometimes Jeff would ride along with the Taylors as they climbed the hills overlooking the lake. And one day he rode with Mr Rudland out of town, past small wooden farmhouses with red tile roofs where Rudland stopped to talk to a farmer feeding his pigs. They had even dismounted at a market and watched an artist painting a design on a large bowl. Jeff would have liked to see a lot more of the country. Trouble was, he couldn't go anywhere by himself. And even with one of the missionaries along, he was stared at and people were always asking questions about him. "How did the young foreigner get such white hair?" and stuff like that. He was better off right here in the yard.

He scooped up a bucket of feed for Gracie to take to the goats tethered in the back yard. Snow still cowered in shaded corners, afraid of the sunshine that coaxed new blades of grass from the bare earth. Spring would come after all — but it would be weeks yet before there was enough grass to keep the goats full and happy.

"These milk-machines here eat more than all the rest of the household put together."

Gracie patted one brown head that nuzzled at her jacket. "Yes, but if it weren't for them we wouldn't have any milk at all and Papa says it's important we have that. Besides," she grinned at Jeff, "some day we may turn around and eat them after all. Then they'll be worth all the trouble."

Jeff hated the taste and smell of goat's milk. He didn't like the butter made from it either, but he had to admit it was good for the kids to have milk from somewhere. "Makes your bones and teeth strong," he told Grace. "Milk has lots of calcium in it."

"Oh, Jeff, you know so much!" she said without trying to hide her admiration.

Jeff shrugged. It wasn't true, probably, but he didn't mind her saying so.

"How do you know all about what food does for you, and how a body works and all that kind of thing?"

Jeff shrugged. "I ... read about it." How could she understand all the knowledge modern science had revealed — up until recently they hadn't even known there were such things as vitamins.

"Papa says you're a big help to him in the clinic. Are you going to be a doctor some day?"

"I don't know. I hadn't exactly planned that far yet. Maybe. I like it. My Dad's a doctor. Sometimes at school we see movies on the circulatory system, CPR techniques, how to do the Heimlich's man-euver for someone who's choking ..." He stopped. Everything he had just said was probably nonsense to Grace, or even to her father for that matter. They'd never seen a film on anything. Nobody had heard of CPR. And Louis Pasteur, he tried to re-member, yes it was about this time that Pasteur was experimenting with pasteurization. But that was in Europe and far removed from them. Yet here they were living normal lives and even practicing medi-cine without knowing any of these things ...

Grace was staring at him, head to one side. "I don't understand you at all, Jeffrey Anderson. You do say the silliest things. But I like you anyway." She turned her big smile on and Jeff grinned back.

"OK. That's good. You don't have to under-stand. Let's tie these fellas up in that other corner and let them graze. Then I've gotta go and help Mr Rudland with the printing press." Jeff left Gracie playing in the shade in her favorite spot — the small private yard behind the stone wall where she was out of curious eyes. The sun barely warmed the stones this early in the year but with her thick padded jacket she was warm. She laid the small cotton-stuffed doll Maria had made for her in the box that served as a doll bed. He could hear her singing as he walked away.

In a small room off the office, Rudland was poring over a box of lead type as Jeff walked in. The heavy press and metal type was a fascinating thing to see and was in constant use. As quickly as Mr Taylor could translate them, portions of the Bible were printed, using western letters instead of Chinese characters. Jeff knew the printing crew would be busier than usual today because it was nearing the deadline for the magazine Hudson Taylor published, called the "Occasional Paper."

"Who reads this, anyway?" Jeff asked.

"Christians in England." Rudland peeled off his jacket and wiped his greasy hands on a rag. "You've probably seen Mr and Mrs Taylor writing articles for it. They write them here, then send them back to England to be published. People who give to our work need to know what their money is being used for."

Jeff stacked a number of pages in a pile as he was told.

"And the people who pray for us want to know that God is answering," Rudland added. He scanned a page for mistakes.

"You mean there are people in England who

really pray for you guys — I mean all of you particularly — every week or something?"

"Aye. Every day in some cases." There was a pause between sentences as Rudland put another metal block of type in place as if he couldn't talk and work at the same time. "They pray for us as individuals or for the Mission work, pray in detail."

He straightened up and rubbed a discolored handkerchief over his wide forehead. "In fact every Saturday, there's a group meets in a home in London to pray for the work here. They want to know what to ask God for and how to thank Him." He shook his head slowly. "I don't know what we'd ever do if people weren't praying for us like that."

Jeff thought he might as well ask what he'd wondered for a long time. "Where do you guys get money from anyway? I know missionaries aren't exactly paid, like by a company or something, but where do you get money to live?"

"From God. Actually, from Christians that God persuades to give to us."

"That's all?"

"That's enough. Mr. Taylor reminds us of that every day. What God chooses to give is enough. He'll never forget what we need or when."

Jeff nodded for lack of a reply.

"Come on. These pages have to be done by tomorrow. Let's get to work."

"How'd you learn how to use this printing press?

Looks kind of complicated."

William Rudland smiled and rubbed large, stubby fingers through his bushy hair. He spoke slowly, deliberately and Jeff had learned to wait a few seconds for his answer to anything.

"Well, I'm learning it as I go along. You see, truth is, I have no tongue for languages. I was near to makin' myself sick trying to learn Chinese. I'm from a blacksmith's family, not educated like Mr Taylor is. I tried my hardest, so I did. But Mr Taylor knew I was having trouble. One day he says to me, 'Go and help the Chinese printers with the presses. They know how to print, they can teach you.' Seems they weren't getting on with things fast enough by themselves. So I came and learned from them."

He took another huge stack of papers from Jeff's arms and laid them on the table. "But d'ye know what happened — and here's the best part — while I do the printing I'm learning Chinese at the same time. It's much easier this way than with my head in a book. You know I think Mr Taylor knew that would happen. I think now," he jabbed a big finger with blackened nails in Jeff's direction and said slowly, " I think he sent me to help with the printing on purpose, not so much for the printing as for me. A good plot it was! I feel better and I'm doing something worthwhile!" He laughed, a loud, deep laugh. "Aye, that Mr Taylor, he's a sharp one, he is."

It was late one Friday night, when Jeff was lying awake in the darkness, that he heard Maria and Hudson Taylor talking softly in the next room.

"We have enough for now, I'm sure. For next week maybe. But we'll be out of rice after that if more money doesn't come soon."

"God will send some by then."

"Maria, you always have the same answer. God will provide. Don't you ever worry, even a little bit? You put me to shame."

"Hudson, you forget I was an orphan with nobody but the Lord to depend on for years before I met you. I learned to trust God then and I've been trusting Him all my life. How can I start to worry now?"

Hudson laughed softly. Then after a minute he continued, "You're right. We're doing God's work. He'll look after us — and it."

"You know what you always tell me, that 'God's work done in God's way will never lack God's supply'."

"I know, I know. And it's true. I still believe it. I just get concerned sometimes. There are so many depending on me …"

"Not on you, Hudson. They're all depending on God just like we are. It's His responsibility."

"Mmm-hmm. You're right again. My absolutely marvelous wife! Sometimes I wonder what I ever did before you came along."

Maria laughed now. "You worried yourself sick

and worked yourself to death, that's what. And shocked all the elderly single lady missionaries in Ningbo with your revolutionary ideas!" There was a muffled laugh. Then Hudson's voice said, "Ideas like working in the interior, and dressing in Chinese clothes — and depending on God for money. Oh, my, what a stir I caused. But I'm glad I won — at least I won you, and that's all that matters."

Maria giggled.

Jeff didn't mean to eavesdrop. It was just that the walls were thin and the night was quiet. But now that he'd heard he couldn't help thinking about it. Something about God's work having God's provision ... From what he'd seen, it seemed Hudson and Maria, and all of them for that matter, really expected that to work. They really seemed to believe that trusting God was enough. Every morning when they gathered for prayer together Jeff heard them tell God what they needed. And every noon for an hour, besides praying for their families at home or the Chinese they were teaching or what to do about some problem, they asked God for whatever they needed. And that was that. Like it was God's responsibility now. Well, God was answering to some extent. At least the whole bunch of them were still eating. But it seemed like God could provide a whole lot more if He wanted to. There sure were a lot of things they didn't have.

The next morning Jeff was crossing the courtyard when he saw Tsiu straining to load some baskets and boxes into a wheelbarrow, while Mr Nicol gave instructions. Jeff had only met Mr Nicol an hour before. He was one of the missionaries with the China Inland Mission but he was working in another town about ten miles away.

"What's going on?" Jeff asked. He noticed that Mr Nicol was wearing English-style clothes, even though Mr Taylor wanted everyone to wear Chinese outfits. Being the only foreigner in a new town like Nicol was in Xiaoshan, it sure would seem safer to look as inconspicuous as possible. Oh well, that was his business.

"I go to preach," Tsiu called to him, smiling broadly. He made it sound as exciting as a Caribbean vacation, a rare treat.

"Tsiu's coming with me," Nicol explained. "We've rented rather good premises in Xiaoshan. Quite suitable really; an apartment upstairs — three rooms — and a room downstairs that we made into a chapel. It's ready for use now and we're going to have the opening ceremony."

"And Mr Tsiu is going to be the speaker?"

"That's right. My Chinese is still inadequate; anyway, having Tsiu will make it a special occasion."

"Good idea. You couldn't prove it by me, but I think he's very good." Jeff and Tsiu exchanged smiles. "In fact, if he sticks around me long enough he'll be able to preach in English as well as Chinese."

"Yes. Well, let's be going," Mr Nicol said. Mr Nicol sure didn't make himself look Chinese like the others did. His foreignness seemed to ooze from him. It wasn't just his overdone accent, it was his attitude, his life, the way he dressed, the way he breathed. Almost like he just wanted to cause trouble. Well, Mr Tsiu didn't seem to notice.

They rolled the loaded cart out the gateway. "Goodbye," Tsiu called to Jeff. "Two days, I come back." He grinned. Jeff had helped expand his English vocabulary since their first limited conversation. At least now they could understand each other.

"Yeah. Have a good time. Preach well." That wasn't the thing to say, but he had to say something. Jeff had no doubt Tsiu was a good preacher. He loved to sit and watch his face and hear the rise and fall of his tones as he explained the posters. He didn't need to understand the words to catch Tsiu's enthusiasm. And the Chinese evangelist never seemed to be too tired to talk to anyone asking about "the Truth" as they called it.

On Sunday the clinic was closed and the household gathered for church services. Every week one or two more Chinese joined them and several wanted to be baptized. There were nearly fifty church members now. On Monday morning the chapel became a waiting room again as the the crowd of patients filled it and overflowed into the yard once more.

Jeff walked into the treatment room Tuesday

morning and put on his gown that had been hanging behind the door.

"Shouldn't we change these?" he asked, looking at the bloodstains on the front from a lip suturing job the day before.

"Not necessary. We had clean ones only yesterday. Even in a big hospital in London they wouldn't be that extravagant."

"Won't we take germs from one patient to another on our gowns?"

"Oh, you sound like Mr Lister. He had that idea a year or so ago. I recall reading about it in a journal my sister sent me." Taylor pulled a bottle marked 'Spirits of Nitre' from the shelf and dusted it off before he continued, "There must be some truth to it, too. He appears to have had some success when it comes to reducing deaths after surgery. Painting the wound with carbolic acid like he did must have some effect."

He mixed a solution of lime chloride in a beaker as he talked. "But it's not for the average doctor. Certainly not for us out here. We have to make do with what's available." He opened a large ledger, ran his finger down to the appropriate spot and made some notes in small script. Jeff had seen him do this often enough to know what it was — the date, the amount of lime chloride used and the amount remaining in the container, to the last tenth of a milliliter.

Jeff said nothing.

"Mind you, I believe in being careful. When I was in medical training they were very strict on hand cleaning. They wouldn't let us go straight from dissecting a cadaver into the delivery room without washing our hands in solution to kill the putrefaction. It was this mixture right here." He motioned to the lime chloride. "That's why I insist on us washing our hands in between patients. A good scrubbing after every patient. I insist on that."

Jeff washed his hands more thoroughly than usual even though the solution felt like it was eating its way through to the bone. He filled the big iron pot with water and set it on the charcoal burner to boil, so they could at least wash the instruments in hot water between patients.

Meanwhile Hudson was using the few spare minutes to pore into the microscope at a blood slide he had made. After looking he opened another huge ledger to the appropriate page and carefully recorded what he saw. He was like that with everything — accurate records, exact details. Jeff wondered if anything could slip by him.

"Do you ever wish you had stayed in England where you could practice medicine in a decent hospital with enough equipment?" Jeff asked one day during a lull in the patient flow.

"Oh, to be honest there's times I wish I had better facilities, more training, so I could do a better job. And I do like to read the new medical journals so I can keep up with what's being discovered. Like that man Lister's finding, for instance. But stay in England? Never." He lifted a thin hand to catch the sweat that was starting to run down his forehead. A smile broke on his face and the weary look vanished suddenly. "I'm where God wants me. Right here. I never doubt that."

Jeff didn't answer. He swept a little pile of dirt out the door and put the broom back in the corner. He knew Hudson Taylor was the best trained medical man around and that meant he was in great demand even though his knowledge was limited. What's more he was often successful.

"One thing I'm learning since I came to China," Hudson was continuing, "is that it's God's work and He'll have to give me all I need to do it. Time, energy, money ... whatever. I do the best I can, in His strength and that's all. But I have to admit I still tend to worry a bit. Maria, now, she just sails along without a doubt. Need something? Trust God. That's that. Myself, I believe it, and I preach that to our team, but sometimes my mind is perplexed to see how it's going to work out."

Jeff remembered the conversation he had overheard a few nights earlier about money being almost gone. It was true, Maria seemed less uptight about the situation than Hudson. And yet, for all the problems he had, Mr Taylor was a lot calmer than Jeff would have expected. His mind quickly snapped back to what Mr Taylor was saying.

"I tell you one thing I wish we had though, some

kind of drug that would treat TB and cholera. I think it won't be long before they find a cure for smallpox, now that they've started experimenting with innoculations. Maybe in a few years that won't be such a threat as it is now. But tuberculosis and cholera they've never found drugs for. Those are killers, Jeffrey. We're helpless against them. If anyone ever finds a cure for those two, it'll save a lot of lives."

"Yes, sir. I'm sure it will."

They were putting away the last of the day's instruments when Maria flung open the door of the clinic and entered. She shoved a piece of paper at Hudson. "The mail came. Look at this. From our dear friend, George Muller."

It took only a moment for Taylor's face to register a reaction.

"A hundred pounds! Oh, Maria, that's wonderful! All we need and more. Oh, thank you, Lord. Thank you. You did it once again, just in time."

"Didn't I tell you, my dear Hudson?" Maria said, laughing as she caught his hand.

"You did, you did. And I agree, God's work done in God's way will never — and I have to underline *never* — lack God's supply."

"By the way, you'd better give some of that to the cook so he can go and buy rice. I didn't want to worry you, but we used the last of it this morning."

It was on Wednesday morning when Jeff went to

the chapel to motion in the next patient that he saw
him again — the thin-faced boy in the ragged blue
jacket with a funny-looking eye. He was peering
through the window. When he saw Jeff he pulled
his head back instantly, but it was too late. Jeff
pushed his way through the crowd and out the
door. Why was that guy always spying on him? He
started to run after him, but in a second the boy had
squeezed out the fence and was gone down the
street. No use trying to catch him now. Oh, well,
he'd probably stay away for today at least. Jeff
snapped off a twig and flung it to the ground. "Get
lost!" he muttered under his breath. "Just get lost."

Staring. They were always staring at him. With
Chinese clothes he didn't get quite as much attention as otherwise, but he still couldn't go out of the
yard without people lining up to watch him pass.
And even here in the compound, the Chinese kids
gawked at him through the fence like he was a
freak. He wished he could just stay out of sight. But
he couldn't. No telling how long he was going to be
here and he had to do something. He sat on the
stairs and watched the activity of the household
going on around him. Didn't these people mind
being stared at? And didn't they ever get homesick?
Or tired? Or sick of the crowds always pushing in
around them? The more he thought about it, the
more miserable he became. Would he ever get
home? He felt tears coming into his eyes and quickly
brushed them away and blinked.

"Hello, Jeff," a voice broke in on his thoughts. "Can you help me with my sums?" It was Gracie, with Bertie tagging along behind.

"Your what?" Jeff quickly brushed his arm across his eyes and took the book she thrust at him. "Oh, addition. Sure. What ones are you doing?" He was glad of the diversion and Grace was a fast learner. Her long, loose curls hung forward, scraping the page as she bent over to work on the problems. He did several examples and encouraged her to do some more. "You'll get it now. Just remember to carry that number," he said, finally. "You do them by yourself now. If I do them for you you'll never learn how."

"Thank you very much, Jeffrey. When I get these finished will you come to the garden with me and see what I did with Elizabeth?"

"With who?"

"Elizabeth. My doll. Remember?"

"Oh, sure. You get your schoolwork done and then I'll go see."

Her smile melted his frustration and anger. He felt warm all the way to his toes.

Just then the gate from the street was thrown open and Mr Nicol strode in. Behind him came Tsiu, limping, his face caked in blood, his pants torn to shreds and stiff where blood had dried in patches. His eyes were swollen almost shut.

Jeff ran to help him. "What happened? Gracie, run and get your Papa."

Jeff felt goosebumps break out on his arms as he listened to the story that came out.

"It was Monday evening that the trouble started," Nicol was explaining, trying hard to keep his agitation under stiff control. The magistrate and fifty or sixty servants had come to Mr Nicol's house, grabbed him and demanded to see his apartment and all his belongings. The magistrate was obviously drunk and seemed unreasonable. "He even refused the tea I offered him as a gesture of friendship. Very rude indeed. He was shouting and ranting."

Nicol's face tightened as he carried on with the explanation.

"Finally, with no warning, the magistrate ordered Tsiu to kneel down. Two of his servants grabbed him — one his hair and one his feet — and threw him to the ground."

Jeff wished he could cover his ears against what he knew was coming. Nicol continued, "Then two others picked up leather straps and began to beat him. First his legs. Six hundred lashes."

Mr Taylor had run out to the yard by now and knelt to examine the mangled legs. Jeff watched, horrified, as Tsiu slowly, painfully, inched up one pant leg. What he saw made his stomach tighten.

He groaned softly, hunched up his shoulders and edged closer to Duncan who was beside him. The warm arm next to his own calmed him. "What a mess!" he whispered. Tsiu winced as Mr Taylor gently touched the puffy, mangled tissue.

"I could hardly stand to see it," Nicol was saying, "but he's a Chinese citizen so I could not interfere."

Tsiu wiped a place on his cheek that was oozing.

"Then they turned him over and began to hit him on the face," Nicol went on. "They gave him fifty lashes on each side."

Maria handed Tsiu a wet cloth with which to dab his eyes. Long red welts marked his swollen face and his lower lip was split open. Jeff could hardly believe anyone would do that to a man for no reason. He fought off the wave of nausea that swept over him. Slowly he sank to the ground beside his friend. What could he say? "I'm sorry"? "Too bad"? "What rotten people"? There was nothing he could say, nothing he could do. He reached out cautiously and took Tsiu's free hand. Maybe that would be enough. Tsiu would understand.

Mr Nicol was continuing "... told us to get out of town that night. Finally they allowed us to stay till this morning but they said we had to leave immediately and anyone who remained would be beheaded. Including our servants. They even beat the landlord for renting to us."

Jeff noticed Mr Taylor stiffen at this. *No wonder*, Jeff thought, *when one of his orders had been deliberately disregarded.*

"Said Christian gospel prohibited in China," Tsiu said slowly through swollen lips.

"Yes. And that goes against the treaty," Nicol

put in indignantly. "The treaty allows us to teach and grants us protection from..."

Jeff didn't want to hear the rest. "I'll get you a drink," he said quickly to Tsiu, and left. He didn't care much about the politics of it and he needed to clear his head. He could see Mr Taylor was angry at Nicol for breaking his part of the agreement. They had promised the landlord that the missionaries renting the property would wear Chinese clothes and live in a Chinese style. Nicol had been asking for trouble by not doing so.

"That's what Tsiu gets for his preaching," he said to Duncan as they met in the kitchen. "Poor guy! And he didn't even commit a crime! Just beaten for no reason. How could anybody do that?"

"He was guilty of being party to a foreign religion. In the people's eyes that's enough to warrant punishment."

"Boy, I wouldn't preach again, if I were him, at least not in a new town where Christians are not welcome."

Duncan smiled and shook his head. "Aach, then you misjudge the man. He'll be preaching again as soon as he can talk properly," he said softly. "That man loves the Lord — he'll not let a beating stop him."

"But there's more to it than meets the eye," the Scotsman continued solemnly. "What Mr Taylor fears — and I agree with him — is that this one incident could be multiplied in all our stations. We've not seen the end yet. This could be the beginning of trouble for all of us."

SIX

Escorting the Skeleton

As the warmer weather came and sunshine mellowed the countryside, no more hostile events occurred and Tsiu's wounds began to heal. Jeff's mind still revolted at the memory of the incident, but at least there seemed to be no further sign of trouble.

Duncan was just coming back from his morning visit to the market when Jeff saw him. "Finished drinking tea for today?"

"Yes. I'll float if I drink another drop, so I will." They laughed but Duncan dropped his voice and said close to Jeff's ear, "There's more rumors."

They said no more till they reached a corner of the kitchen where Maria was spooning food into the baby's mouth. Then Duncan went on, "I think there's more suspicion aroused about us. I've been talking to the men in the tearoom down the street. They were very polite to me, asked the usual questions about my honorable name and age and occupation and so on, and when I told them I was a teacher of the 'True Way' they listened politely. But after I left several men accosted me on the way home and wanted to know what we did with the children we kidnaped."

"What? What children?" Jeff asked, shocked. "Where did they get the idea you kidnaped anybody?"

"It's a common belief." Duncan wiped his forehead with a handkerchief before going on. "They say we kidnap women and children, cut them open and sell their organs. But now there's a new rumor. Supposedly we killed seven children recently and salted them down to preserve the bodies. Supposedly they are buried here some place."

Jeff laughed. It was so ridiculous he wondered how anyone could believe it.

"Oh, I heard a better one than that," Maria put in. "We captured a little girl here and cut out her kidneys. When she died her mother was not too happy with the idea, so we placated her with a gift of $20 and a big feast!"

"Wow! These people will believe anything," Jeff said. "Where do they get these ideas anyway?"

"The stories are started — or at least fed — by the magistrates who want to make trouble so the mandarins will kick out all the foreigners living in their district. Most of the rumors don't amount to anything."

"True," Duncan said. "But I'm not so easy about these. This time the people seem a bit more edgy, a bit suspicious."

"But look how they flock to the clinic every day," Jeff pointed out. "Surely they wouldn't come if they were really scared of having their kidneys cut out or something."

"Well, some of them don't believe all they hear. And I guess some are so desperate they have to take a chance. And some probably come just to keep an eye on us and see for themselves."

Jeff perked up. "Hey, maybe that's why that kid keeps peeking in here. Maybe he's trying to see what we're doing with the patients. Or maybe he thinks I've been kidnaped by you and he wants to check every day if I'm still alive."

"What kid? Who are you talking about?" Duncan asked.

"Oh, nothing. There's just this boy that keeps bugging me — always sticking his face around the gate or in the window, and when I look at him he runs. He doesn't say anything. Just looks and looks. Drives me crazy."

"Well, don't let it bother you," Duncan advised him. "Lots of people want to see what goes on here, and we mustn't mind. After all, that's the only way they'll learn to trust us."

"Maybe when they see that we don't saw people

in half or something, their suspicions will be laid to rest," Maria added. "But we'd better be on our guard not to give them anything to get alarmed about for the time being, until the rumors die down."

"Don't worry, I'll be sure to keep my knife and my salt shaker out of sight," Jeff said, grinning.

It was a few days later that Hudson Taylor called Duncan and Jeff into his office and closed the door behind them.

"We've got a problem, gentlemen," Taylor said, rubbing his chin. "I looked through these boxes that came from Shanghai the other day and discovered that one I had intended to be stored there for future use has been sent by mistake. Come and look at this."

Making sure they were alone he motioned them to a closet, where a large wooden crate about the size of a storage trunk lay opened on the floor. Hudson Taylor lifted the wrapper on top. Jeff's mouth dropped open. It was a human skeleton. It had leg bones, joints, sets of teeth, a skull, all carefully packed. He reached out gingerly and touched one. It was a display model like in the biology lab for teaching anatomy in health class.

Duncan began to smile, then a broad grin spread across his whole face. "So this is where you've been keeping all the poor unfortunate victims you've poisoned. Even took them to pieces, bone by bone, did you?" He chuckled.

Hudson Taylor smiled and a twinkle came to his

eye. "Yes. Exactly. That's exactly what people will think. The children we supposedly salted and preserved? Here they are, right in our house like they claim. I had no idea this was here. I brought it out from England hoping to do some teaching later on. It wasn't meant to be sent to us — at least not yet. But here it is. You can see if the mandarin comes searching the place and finds this, we're in for trouble."

"You could just dig a hole and bury it for a while," Jeff suggested. "Then dig it up when you want it."

Taylor shook his head. "Won't do. Everyone will know we buried a box — the servants will tell in no time — and that will be even harder to explain. They'll be sure we're guilty then."

"I guess you could throw it in the river," Duncan said. "Although that has the same risk. If anyone saw us — and who can do anything without being seen? — they'd immediately be suspicious."

"No, there's only one thing to be done," Mr Taylor concluded. "I want you to take this box to Ningbo. It'll be safe there with my friends until the whole accusation business blows over."

Duncan said nothing for a moment or two. His sandy-colored bushy eyebrows wiggled up and down before he spoke. "You know how dangerous this is," he said finally. "If anyone on the boat questions us we're in trouble. What if someone makes us open the box?"

Taylor nodded. "I know. There's that possibility. But there's no other choice. It's less risky than
any other option. You can go with him, Jeff," he
said. "The trip will be interesting for you and Duncan
will need the company."

Jeff was excited about the possibility of a trip by
river boat to another city. But he was less thrilled
about trying to smuggle out a box of bones without
being caught.

Still, when the next morning dawned, Jeff was
ready. His flesh prickled with excitement — and
fear — as he buttoned his Chinese jacket and
tiptoed downstairs. First time he'd ever escorted a
coffin! It was barely light when he and Duncan
slipped out of the house.

The city was still half-asleep. *Good thing*, Jeff
thought. *The less people see of us the better.*
Looking as nonchalant as possible, they rolled the
cart with its plain-looking box slowly along the
narrow streets toward the city gate.

"Halt!" The guard at the city wall stopped them.
He called out a sharp command or two and Duncan stepped forward. Jeff stood by the cart fidget-
ing while they talked. He felt his stomach tighten-
ing up. What was the guy saying? *What if he
wants to see what we've got? Maybe we could
pretend it's — forget it! What can you pretend
about a skeleton*! There was no way they could
disguise it or excuse it. "Oh, God, please," Jeff
prayed quickly. "Make them let us pass without

any trouble."

Duncan was showing the guard his foreign pass-port now. They talked a bit longer and Jeff saw the guard smile. The two bowed to each other and separated on apparently friendly terms.

"Whew!" Jeff said when he and Duncan were safely rolling again. "I was afraid we were in for trouble before we ever get out of town."

"Aye, rightly so. But he never asked to see our load. I thank God for that. Now let's hope we can get a boat as easily."

The river was a fascinating place, Jeff thought, and obviously well-used. It was probably as impor-tant for transport as the interstate highways back home. Dozens of small flat boats, like barges, car-ried passengers and goods up and down. The weathered looking boatmen, sweat glistening on their bare backs and sinewy arms, poled the boats along the bank. At just the right spot, they skillfully maneuvered their craft out into the current.

Jeff watched the scene as he stayed with the cart containing their strange cargo, aiming at looking inconspicuous, while Duncan tried to get passage for them on a departing boat. He was sure glad he had let Mr Taylor talk him into dressing in Chinese clothes — he'd stick out like a sore thumb in jeans and a teeshirt.

"Let's go," Duncan said, returning at last. "One man has agreed to take us without charging an arm and a leg."

Jeff laughed. "If he did, I've got a few here for him."

Duncan smiled and winked. "Hush. We mustn't arouse their suspicions."

The boat had more than its share of passengers. Jeff squeezed into a spot near the middle. At one side four or five boisterous men laughed and shouted, elbowing their way to a comfortable spot. Jeff recognized by their uniforms that they were soldiers.

A couple of merchants sat nearby, their wares loaded in bamboo baskets. In one corner two thin men sprawled weakly on thin mats, coughing. Ignoring the oncoming passengers and the commotion of loading they puffed occasionally from long-stemmed pipes and drifted back into a silent stupor.

"Opium smokers," Duncan said, nodding in their direction.

By the anchor mounting a prisoner sat chained to a burly-looking guard, over to the left were a couple of younger people Jeff thought were students, and to the right was a man of high rank with his servants whom he kept busy performing one errand after another.

Everyone looked at the two foreigners curiously when they first got on, and a few asked the usual questions. But after Duncan had apparently answered satisfactorily, most went back to their own affairs.

Jeff stretched into as much space as possible, stuffing his jacket under him to soften the wooden floor. They made good speed. The sun was warming now and Jeff would have enjoyed himself, but he couldn't shake that uneasy feeling. Who was that man beside Duncan anyway? No one else seemed particularly suspicious about the two "foreign devils" traveling with a long box. But that one bothered Jeff. He was well-dressed and seemed polite — probably a nobleman or government official. *Just what we don't need*, Jeff groaned, *a high-ranking bureaucrat of some kind asking questions.* He wished Duncan wouldn't lead him into conversation.

As night fell, the banter and babble on board died down. Jeff found by a little wiggling and squashing he could lie down between Duncan and the box, although he had no room to stretch his legs full length. He could hardly keep his eyes open, but he was afraid to let them close. Being surrounded by people who could at any minute become enemies gave him an edgy feeling. No explanation would save their necks if anyone discovered they were carrying bones, even phony ones. Even if they just got suspicious without seeing the evidence, they could cause a nasty incident.

The well-dressed man Duncan had been talking to got up and wiggled his legs to improve circulation. Jeff peeked from under one eyelid. The man stepped over a sleeping body or two and stood by the boat's edge, exchanging a few words with one of the soldiers. Was he alerting the soldier to the foreigners with their suspicious cargo? Then he walked slowly back towards Jeff, stepping carefully over fellow passengers.

Jeff felt his heart racing. He couldn't swallow. He lay deadly still, pretending to be asleep but keeping one eye open.

The gentleman approached, then stopped beside the wooden chest.

Jeff froze every muscle. *Mustn't let him know you're watching,* he told himself. The moon gave enough light for Jeff to see the man reach out one hand and feel silently around the edge of the box. As his fingers ran along the surface, the light glanced off one very long nail on the little finger of his right hand — a sure sign that this man was some kind of VIP. The fingers felt the latch on the box lid.

Jeff's hand clenched into a fist inside his jacket. What would they do if he started prying? Of course the box was locked and tied, but any load had to be opened for inspection if required. Jeff began to pray, "Lord, please keep him from asking questions about the box. Don't let him get suspicious. Please ..." Only God could do anything about a situation like this.

The man was looking intently at the label giving destination and name of sender. Mr Taylor had written it in his best Chinese script, hoping it would look unremarkable. The gentleman read it carefully by moonlight, and Jeff waited for his next move.

As the minutes ticked by, Jeff felt himself drifting

off to sleep. He tried desperately to keep an eye open. The man was sitting down now, leaning against the box, his back to Jeff. Was he planning a strategy to get the box open? Was he sending secret signals to the soldier he had talked with earlier? Jeff couldn't be sure. His eyes would not stay open any longer. Gradually sleep overcame him.

The noise on the boat increased before sunrise and Jeff shook himself awake. He was stiff and chilly. Then he remembered. The box.

He propped himself up on one elbow and had a look. Still there. Unopened. And the high-class gentleman seemed to have disappeared.

"Hey, where did that guy go?" he asked Duncan. "The one who was snooping around the box half the night."

"He got off during the night," Duncan said, smiling. "We stopped briefly at a town a few miles back and the man got off. You were sound asleep."

"Well, I'm glad he's gone. I was scared stiff he was going to ask to examine our 'bones' here. Who was he anyway?"

Duncan chuckled and his thick eyebrows puckered together. "An educated gentleman and very polite. But it's good he didn't get suspicious about our cargo. That man," he said seriously now, "was a high-ranking employee of the mandarin."

Jeff gulped. The mandarins were not exactly overjoyed at having foreigners living in their midst.

This guy would only have to breathe a word to his boss ... With a rush of relief Jeff realized how close they had come to trouble. He caught the gleam in Duncan's eye. "An employee of the mandarin. Right beside us all that way! God was sure helping us on that one!" He shook his head and smiled. Then laughed. And next thing he knew he and Duncan were both laughing, letting all the tensions of the last few hours roll off.

"We'll be at Ningbo pretty soon now. Then we can get rid of Mr Phony Bones here and breathe easy again."

Jeff was glad when it was all over a few hours later. The box was delivered safely, and they had stopped for a meal of noodles. Now the boat for the return journey had nearly finished loading.

"Mr Taylor will be glad to hear we accomplished our mission successfully," Duncan said, slapping Jeff on the back playfully. "Come on, let's get back to Hangzhou — just you and me this time, without our bony friend."

"Maybe that'll end the silly stories about us. There's absolutely nothing they could find to prove any of the stuff they say, especially now that we've gotten rid of the skeleton. Think the rumors will die down?"

"I don't know, Jeff. I'd not be so sure if I were you. We'll see; we'll see."

SEVEN

Assaults and Alarms

"Look at this," Mr Taylor said to Jeff as he sat down for breakfast. He held out a large rock. "This was thrown over the wall last night. Did you hear the commotion?"

"No, I sleep like a log. I didn't hear a thing. Who would do that?"

"I don't know, but it isn't the first time. You see that pile of rocks beside the garden wall over there?" He pointed to the area where Gracie played. "They have all been thrown during the past several nights, aimed at us and our windows. None did any damage, praise the Lord. But that incident with Nicol and Tsiu wasn't an isolated case and it wasn't the end of the matter."

Duncan agreed. "It was worse than that at the homes of other missionaries. Mr Green and the

Valentines have had their share of opposition, and last night at the Kreyers' home they almost broke down the gate."

A couple of hours later Jeff saw Mr Taylor leaving his study, dressed in very unusual clothes. His head was covered with a broad-brimmed flat silk hat, topped with a gold button from which hung a long red tassel, reaching down to his shoulders. His gown was blue brocade, padded and embroidered with gold silk threads and tied at the waist. On top of that he wore a short brown satin jacket and, on his feet, black satin shoes. The whole picture reminded Jeff of the Chinese lord he had seen in the movie *Marco Polo*.

"I'm going to see the mandarin," Taylor announced.

"Neat outfit," Jeff said approvingly. "I like that hat. Especially the big gold egg on the top."

Taylor laughed. "The button one wears is very important. Indicates rank, you know. Sort of like stripes on a military uniform. The top ranking one is a plain red button for ministers of state. Then an opaque red stone, often engraved with fancy designs, for a viceroy. He's the equivalent of a duke or earl in England." Taylor listed off the order on his fingers as he talked. "Then, let's see, it's the deep blue ... yes, the provincial governor wears a deep blue gem. The next rank down is a light blue gem; the city prefect wears crystal, the magistrate an opaque white stone. And lastly, ourselves. The gold button is the rank of anyone subordinate to the magistrate. An educated man, perhaps, but with no nobility."

Jeff was amazed. Taylor had memorized every detail of Chinese protocol. No one could say he didn't try!

"Now, Tsiu, come show me again," Taylor called. "How low am I supposed to bow to this honorable gentleman?"

Tsiu came hurrying in, laughing. "Like this, like this," he said, bending to the precise angle. "Now try. Very important." He gave a couple more lessons in official behavior before he scurried off to answer the door gong.

"I think the best course of action is a bold one," Hudson Taylor explained to Jenny and Emily. Maria stood beside him nodding agreement. Taylor went on, retying his sash to create a perfect impression, "A couple of other missionaries, Mr Green and Mr Valentine, are going with me. We hoped we wouldn't have to, but the atmosphere is getting more uneasy. And now this latest rock-throwing incident. It's time to take action. If we all stick together and let the mandarin know we expect his cooperation, maybe he'll put a stop to the rumors and abuse."

"I'm sure that's the best course, dear," Maria answered, jostling the infant Maria on one hip. "At least that way they won't feel we are doing anything in secret. Best to be open with them."

"I do want Nicol to get permission to live in

Xiaoshan again. But it's not just for his sake or ours, but for all the missionaries in the future as well. So much depends on the attitude of the officials."

When the other two Englishmen had arrived they climbed in sedan chairs and pulled away, headed for the yamen, the mandarin's official residence. The sunshine was warm on Jeff's back as he watched them go. He peeled off his jacket. "I guess I was wrong about never being warm again," he said to Gracie. "It can get hot here in a hurry."

The crowd was growing in the waiting room and courtyard when Taylor got back in the afternoon, but he walked on by them into the sitting room. He called the household together to tell them what had happened.

"The mandarin wouldn't see us at first. Kept us waiting for an hour or more. We knew if we left without seeing him, people would immediately realize we were not welcomed by the officials, and that would give them leave to do whatever they wanted. So after a long while Mr Green said to me — said it very loudly and deliberately, mind you, so the servants would hear — 'Well, Taylor, we might as well go, but it sure is too bad to have all the bother of going through our countries' consuls to conduct business when we might have spoken to the top man directly and avoided an international incident.' Well, that did it. You should have seen those officers scurry off. In no time at all, they said the mandarin would see us."

Maria grinned. "That's the way to go about things! He wouldn't want the embarrassment of having the British ambassador causing a scene. So did he listen to you?"

"Oh, yes. In fact he gave us every courtesy. Ushered us into a reception room with the prefect himself." Mr Taylor laughed just recalling the incident. "We had to keep ourselves from chuckling, you know. We remembered our lessons well and sat on the least honorable seats on the right hand side."

Mr Tsiu smiled broadly. "Very good. Very good. Mr Taylor good pupil."

"After everybody was seated correctly and said the right things, we presented our case. We told him our wives and children were in danger, reminded him of the international accords which guarantee us safety and so on. We told him about the clinic too. He really approved of that, especially since it's free to the poor.

"Another funny thing, he likes horses, it seems. Mr Valentine told him how we love to ride for exercise and that caught the prefect's ear immediately. He smiled and nodded and softened up to us all. He said riding a horse, or walking, is fine in the daytime but we should ride a sedan chair after dark. Anyway, eventually he promised to make a statement in our favor and assured us we will have no more trouble. Even escorted us personally to our sedan chairs. Oh, that reminds me." He reached into the bag he had been carrying and gently pulled out a bright pink flower with deep red center. He handed it to Maria. "Picked this for you on the way home. First hibiscus I've seen this season."

Maria stuck the flower in her hair and thanked him. "It's beautiful. Now finish the story."

"Oh yes. Well, escorting us out like that publicly should be proof enough to the whole city that we are innocent. I think the trouble will die down now."

The next day, Jeff heard the usual noise from the crowd in the courtyard suddenly fade. He stuck his head out of the clinic door as the people began to move to one side, looking towards the figure sweeping through the gate. Tsiu pushed past Jeff in his haste to give the news to Mr Taylor. He was wringing his hands as he spoke.

"The prefect's personal secretary is here to see you." Tsiu's agitated face told Jeff this was no ordinary visit.

Taylor strode calmly out of the clinic and greeted the man politely, remembering his bow from the day before. The presence of such an honorable personage could be intended as an honor. It could also be a spying mission. He would have to be shown everything in the place.

Jeff could feel the tension mount among the missionaries as Taylor walked the prestigious guest through the courtyard to the parlor, the dining room, the chapel, treatment room, kitchen ... all over the house he escorted the gentleman. They went upstairs. Jeff knew without following that they were moving from room to room inspecting every foreign wonder. Maria and Miss Blatchley exchanged glances. A few minutes later the two men descended the stairs and Mr Taylor suggested to Jeff, "Come on with us. We'll show the man the printing press."

A few minutes' demonstration satisfied the secretary about its usefulness; then it was on to the laundry. Here Maria's big rollers for ironing sheets were an attraction. Then it was back to the main sitting room, where Mr Taylor took a thermometer from the shelf and showed it to the amazed man. What a wonder, that these numbers could actually tell how hot or cold it was! Finally, as unexpectedly as he had come, the man was gone.

"When you think about it, I guess a thermometer is quite amazing," Jeff admitted to Hudson Taylor as they discussed it later. "Do you think he liked what he saw?"

"Definitely. He was very cordial, and very impressed. In fact, as he left he requested that Nicol go back to Xiaoshan."

"You mean they're willing to rent a house to a foreigner?"

"Apparently. Maybe our troubles are over — for now."

It was at that moment that Tsiu came running in from the couryard. "Mr Taylor, come quick quick.

Very sick man. He die. Come."

Jeff and Duncan followed Taylor as he ran to the treatment room. A thin dark-skinned man lay naked to the waist, stretched out on the table where he had been carried by relatives.

The scene was one of confusion. The man seemed to be in a deep coma. He was motionless, his eyes closed, his chest not moving. *He's dead already,* thought Jeff. Miss Blatchley moved quickly and silently to the cupboard, getting out the things she knew Taylor would need before he even asked. The patient's family cried and wailed, hovering over the victim till Taylor insisted they move away and give him air.

"Can I help?" Jeff asked.

"Here, shine this light in his eyes and see if you can see the pupil get smaller," Taylor instructed him. "I'll get him a stimulant."

Jeff could see no change in the man's eyes. He tried again. *Maybe I'm just not looking for the right thing,* he thought. *I've never done this before.* "I don't see any change," he called to Mr Taylor.

"You're quite right," Taylor said after trying for a few minutes. "There is no reaction. He is severely sedated — in a coma really. I think it's an overdose of opium."

While he worked he talked to the patient's family, who answered his questions with loud descriptions and hand motions. Jeff could see they were telling him something urgent.

"Oh, no," Hudson Taylor said under his breath. "The man's taken a lethal dose. In fact ..." he paused, figuring out something, "what he's had is about three times enough to kill him."

Jeff's mouth dropped open. "Three times! Then he hasn't got a chance, has he?"

"I don't know," Taylor answered softly, injecting another dose of drug into the man's skinny forearm. "There's always a chance. Always. God is not dead."

Jeff was silent. Yeah. He hadn't thought of that. God is not dead. Still ...

A movement at the window caught the corner of his eye. He looked up to see a familiar thin face peering in. The shock of thick black hair hung down the middle of the forehead as usual. *Go away,* Jeff thought. *Go away. Get lost. I don't need you sticking your head in here about now.* But the face didn't move. The eyes were taking in every action, watching every frantic effort to bring some sign of life back into the motionless form.

As the night wore on, Mr Taylor and Miss Blatchley continued to work over the man. Jeff stayed to help as long as he could. "We must try to keep him awake," Miss Blatchley said, slapping the man's cheeks and repeating something to him in Chinese. "Here, try washing his face with this."

Jeff was so occupied with the case he hardly noticed when the face at the window disappeared and emerged a moment later as a quiet figure slipping inside the clinic. The boy stayed close to the door, watching every move yet ready to flee at any moment. Jeff looked at him and went on back to his task. *Let him look,* he decided. *We don't have time to worry about him right now.*

It was after midnight when Mr Taylor sent Jeff off to get some sleep. "We'll take turns with him. You can come back and help in the morning." Jeff didn't argue. He couldn't stand up any longer. He paused on his way out the door and turned to look at the boy huddled in the corner, blue jacket pulled up around his thin face. The boy stiffened, suddenly alert, ready to run. He flattened himself against the dark shadows of the wall as Jeff walked past. His eyes were filled with terror as they peered out at Jeff. For just a second Jeff wanted to say something, to tell him not to be so scared. He hesitated only briefly, then turned and walked up to bed.

Jeff slept lightly. A mosquito buzzed around his ears. He dreamed about the man in the clinic. Skinny. Beads of sweat on his forehead. He rolled over. The mosquito buzzed again. His mind seemed to carry on the drama without him. Three times the lethal dose. Three times. Must get his breathing stronger. Opium. Three times the lethal dose. He swatted a mosquito and shifted his legs. The boy. He sat cowering in the shadows. Watching. Watching. Finally Jeff drifted into oblivion. Next thing he knew was the morning sun poking its way through the cracks in the shutter. He scrambled up quickly, threw on his clothes and ran to the clinic.

A weary Mr Taylor sat beside the sleeping man, hand on his pulse. He looked up as Jeff entered. "Good morning, Jeff. I'm glad to see you. I'll let you sit with our friend here a few minutes while I take a breath of fresh air."

Jeff hardly dared ask. "How is he?"

"Alive. Barely. But he's breathing normally now, at least, and his pulse is stronger. He'll make it, thank God."

A noise behind Jeff made him jump. He turned to see the boy of the night before, huddled in the corner, staring at him silently.

"Has he been here all night?" he asked Mr Taylor, pointing to the blue hump in the shadows.

Mr Taylor nodded and smiled slightly. "He's keeping an eye on me to see what we really do with our patients. From all the rumors he's heard, he's scared to death, but he's not leaving till he sees the end result, I guess." Then he added, "But he did doze off during the night for a couple of hours."

Jeff grinned. "Good. Now he's seen that you didn't eat the guy or cut his heart out, maybe he'll be satisfied."

The kid's brave, Jeff thought. *He was scared to death to be there, but somehow he kept coming. I've got to hand it to him — he's brave. At least he's willing to check us out rather than just run away and believe every rumor he hears. I wonder what it's going to take to convince him we're not ogres?* The boy was watching Jeff now, taking in every detail of his activity. Jeff returned his gaze. For a moment they looked at each other. The Chinese face was wary, carefully concealing any emotion. Slowly, Jeff let a smile creep across his face.

The boy looked at Jeff in confusion, bewilderment replacing some of the terror in his eyes. Gradually his face softened in a tense, uneasy smile, then he turned quickly and bolted for the door.

Mr Taylor had watched in silence. Now he put his hand on Jeff's shoulder. "It's hard for you, isn't it. I know how you feel. You did the right thing, just smiling at him."

Jeff nodded. He turned to gather up Mr Taylor's instruments. "I guess as long as he insists on hanging around we'd better get used to each other."

EIGHT

Gracie

The days moved from spring into summer, increasingly hot and sticky. The air hung motionless and breezeless over the city. Mosquitoes loved it. Jeff did not.

"Do you know the thermometer reads 102 degrees right now in my room?" Mr Rudland announced wearily, wiping his face with an already-saturated handkerchief. "That wouldn't be so bad in the middle of the afternoon, but I don't think it cooled off more than a few degrees all night long."

Maria nodded. "I know. This room here on the shady side is the coolest room in the house and look — even here it's 98°."

Through the month of July and into August the heat persisted. There was little sleep at night, no appetite during the day, and plenty of disease going around all the time.

Bertie pushed away his lunch after only two mouthfuls of rice. "I don't want any more, Mama," he whined. "I'm thirsty, that's all."

"I'm afraid Bertie's sick now too," Maria said after he had been excused to go and lie down. Gracie had been tired and not eating for several weeks. "He was awake half the night," she added. "I hope it isn't from the dog bite he got last month."

Jeff knew about the dog bite on Herbert's cheek but had dismissed it from his mind. Now he began to think — what if it was rabies? Would it start like this? Would Hudson Taylor have any medicine for it? He tried to remember — rabies vaccine, invented by Louis Pasteur in ... when was it? He had no idea. But they must not have it yet or Maria would be using it for Bertie. He didn't want to ask.

"Hi, Bertie," he said later that day, kneeling beside the little boy's bed. "I hear you're sick. I'm sorry. Want me to read to you?"

Bertie tossed restlessly and grabbed Jeff's hand. "Sit down. Stay with me a little while. You can read or sing or do whatever you want, but stay here.   Will you?"

"Sure, Bertie, I'll stick around a while."

"My head aches, Jeffrey. It aches real badly. And I'm too hot. But when I take my covers off I get so cold I shiver."

"That's because you've got a pretty high fever, Bertie. It is too hot though, for all of us. I guess that doesn't help any. Here, let me wet this cloth and wash you off a bit."

Jeff pumped until the water from the well was as cool as possible, then he poured some into a basin and took it up to Bertie's room. He wet a washcloth in the water, wrung it out and spread it over the little boy's forehead.

"There, that might help. My mom does that for me when I get a fever. Feel better?"

Bertie nodded. "Am I going to die, Jeffrey? Do you think I'm so sick I'm going to die?"

Jeff shook his head. What a question! "No, Bertie, you'll get better. You're a tough guy. You'll soon be up and bothering me again as usual." He smiled and Bertie's face lit up in a weak response.

"Good. I don't mind going to see Jesus, you know, but I don't want to go yet. I've got to help Papa and Mama — they need me."

"Sure they do. Don't worry, you'll be here to help for a long time yet." Jeff wasn't sure if that was true or not, but what else could he say? *I hope you're right, Jeff,* he told himself. As the hours passed and Bertie didn't improve he began to wonder.

"I don't know who I'm more concerned about," Hudson Taylor said that evening. "Herbert or

Gracie. Or you, Maria. You're worse than they are."

"No, I'm all right. Just very tired. And hot."

"Yes, and with the children ill you can't sleep, so you can't hope to get better that way. We'll have to get away. A few days up in the mountains would do us all good. How about a vacation in Pengshan?"

"Oh, that would be lovely. Yes, let's go. I'll get things ready while you see if you can find a boat or two to take us."

The mountain village of Pengshan was beautiful. Cool mists rose from the hilltop in early morning, revealing pagodas of fragile beauty and fields of lush green. Rhododendrons and camellias covered the hillside with pink and lavender blooms. Jeff took a deep breath as they stepped ashore.

"Look at that rhododendron, Maria," Hudson said immediately. He picked a large magenta bloom carefully and studied its petals. "I don't think I've seen this variety before. It's different from the Rhododendron macrophyllum ... see how much taller they are?"

Jeff nodded along with Maria. It didn't seem all that unusual, but then he didn't pretend to know anything about flowers. Anyway Mr Taylor noticed details that other people missed. He'd probably enter this new find in his diary, Jeff thought, shaking his head. He looked at Maria who seemed to read his mind. She winked.

The procession began its trek up the hill.

Gracie walked ahead, holding Mr Taylor's hand. Jeff noticed how her feet dragged as they climbed the steep stone path; it wasn't like Gracie not to be running on ahead. A few yards from the path a workman struck a chisel with a heavy thud. "Let's stop a minute, Papa," Gracie said, out of breath. "I'm tired, and I want to watch the man."

The party following them slowed to a halt. Jeff could see the man working under a shed. Looked like he was carving something out of stone.

"What's he making, Papa?" Gracie asked.

"I'm afraid he's carving an idol, Gracie. He's making a stone idol for people who come here to worship."

Jeff looked on with interest. He wondered what the face would look like when the nose was finished.

Gracie came over to him and pulled his sleeve anxiously. "Jeffrey, that man's making an idol."

"Yeah, I see. I'd like to know ..."

"An idol! Papa," Gracie turned to Mr Taylor now, "he doesn't know anything about Jesus or he'd never do it. He wouldn't make idols if he knew. Why don't you tell him, Papa. Tell him, please."

The whole entourage had to wait while Mr Taylor, with Gracie still holding his hand, talked to the man in Chinese and gave him a piece of paper. Probably part of Luke or John, Jeff thought. Jeff sat down on a rock to wait. Did they have to stop and preach now just because some guy was carving an idol? This was supposed to be their vacation! He took the piece of candied ginger Maria offered him. No sense getting impatient; there would be no moving until Mr Taylor finished.

After a few minutes they returned to the path. Gracie seemed satisfied. "We told him," she said to Jeff. "I hope God doesn't punish the man for making an idol ... he didn't know any better."

"Okay. Turn around and get going. We've got to climb all the way up there yet," Jeff said, waving her up the hill. "Let's go."

At the top there was only a derelict temple with three or four rooms still useable, but the priest was friendly and willing to let them stay. So between the temple and three tumbledown sheds the group set up camp. Butterflies flitted in and out among the bushes, and by the second day Mr Taylor had found two more to add to his collection. Even the primitive conditions didn't spoil the fun and in a few days everyone was improving. Everyone except Freddie and Gracie.

"Gracie's fever never seems to go down," Maria said wearily. "I was up with her most of the night." She drew her thin hand across her forehead and sank down onto a stone bench. "She's complaining of her head aching so much. I need more water to sponge her off." Maria sighed and dropped her head onto her chest.

"I'll get some," Jeff volunteered. "You sit here and rest." He took the bucket and headed to the stream for a refill.

When he had returned with the water he looked in on Freddie who was lying on a cot in the big inner room. Just as it looked like Bertie might be recovering, now Freddie was getting worse. The little boy looked at him with glassy eyes. Suddenly, while Jeff watched, Freddie started to twitch and shake all over.

"Help! Mr Taylor, Maria. Somebody." Jeff called running out to the porch. "It's Freddie. He's shaking."

Mr Taylor hurried to the bedside. "Convulsions. Comes from high fever sometimes. Get some cold wet cloths and put them on his head and arms."

Shaking all over, Jeff did as he was told. He'd never seen anybody have convulsions before. It was horrible. He tried to keep his mind on what he could do to help. His heart pounded wildly.

Carefully Taylor pried open the boy's mouth. "Put something between his teeth so he won't bite his tongue with his convulsing," he said to Jeff. "All you can do is wait till it passes."

Gradually the little body quieted and relaxed. Gently Mr Taylor straightened him out on the bed, smoothed his damp hair and shirt, and waved a paper back and forth over him to create a breeze. "He's sleeping now," he said to Jeff. "Best thing he can do. We'll just leave him alone a few hours. He'll sleep."

Taylor sat on the edge of his son's bed and dropped his head onto his hands. How many nights had it been since he'd had a good sleep? *He needs to be in bed himself,* Jeff thought. He had never seen so much sickness in one place. Even when he and Greg both had chicken pox at home it was nothing like this. And to make it worse there was nothing anyone could *do.* Well, except pray, of course. Everyone did a lot of that during the next few days. It seemed kind of natural to stretch out the devotional time after breakfast each morning, with so much sickness to pray about.

Jeff was glad to do what he could to help. Back and forth he went to carry water, get food, help in the kitchen, keep the well children entertained. He and Tsiu were kept running for the next few days. Everyone was doing more than his share of the chores. But still there seemed always to be someone needing something. Sometimes he could hear Mr Taylor himself moaning in his room. He was sick, too, and wouldn't admit it, Jeff knew. So was Maria.

Only thing about being here instead of Hangzhou was the cooler temperature and fresher air. At least when he got a chance, Jeff could fall asleep and wake up refreshed.

As often as he could, he sat beside Gracie. At first she had been glad to have him joke with her, glad to listen to him talk. Now she just lay with her eyes closed, struggling to breathe. Jeff wasn't sure if she even knew he was around her. He reached for her hand. So hot. So thin and hot. He wished there was something he could do — anything.

"Is it meningitis?" Jeff heard Maria whisper to Hudson as they sat by Gracie's bed one day in late August. The girl's long hair had been cut short and cold compresses were piled around her neck constantly.

"I don't know. Could be that or typhus."

It didn't matter. They had no medicine for either one. And the bubbly little eight year old was definitely not getting better. Between convulsions she struggled to breathe. Long into the night Jeff could hear her babbling incoherently, gasping and tossing, struggling for every breath. He lay awake, listening. If only there was something he could do. He felt so helpless.

The moonbeams filtered through the broken walls, hitting him square in the eye. Might as well get up and get a drink.

He tiptoed out past the sleeping household. He glanced in on Gracie as he passed her cot. Emily was sitting beside her, wearily. He went on, out the door, stepping more firmly now, down to the spring. He'd just pump up a drink and go back to bed.

The sound of voices made him stop. Mr Taylor

must be talking to Maria. When Jeff thought about it, it was the only time the Taylors could have any privacy. The sentence he heard stopped him in his tracks.

"Maria, we might as well face it ... we're going to lose our little girl. There's nothing I can do."

A weary voice mumbled, "I know. I've been afraid of that." The sound of Maria's sobs jolted him to action. He shouldn't be hearing this. He turned and retraced his steps. As he left he heard Hudson's voice, broken by tears, saying, "Oh, Heavenly Father, we give you our little Gracie ..."

Jeff hurried back to bed and crawled under the covers without waking the boys. "Dear Heavenly Father, please heal Gracie. I don't think I've asked this before because I thought she'd get better, but ... Please, Lord. I know you healed people before. Please do it now for Gracie. And for Mr and Mrs Taylor's sake. Thank you. In your name, Amen."

The next day, Gracie seemed unchanged. Jeff prayed for her a couple more times, in between all the chores he found to do. He noticed a letter on the table, half-finished, in Mr Taylor's neat handwriting. He couldn't help glancing at it as he passed. "Dear Mr Berger, I am trying to pen a few lines from the couch on which my darling little Gracie lies dying."

He didn't read what followed. How could Mr

Taylor say that, just write a letter talking like that ... Just then Emily called to him and he remembered his errand. The hours dragged. That evening, Mr Taylor called softly to everyone, "Come on in. Everyone gather around. Let's sing."

Jeff was surprised. He thought Mr Taylor was going to tell them Gracie was dying, but he asked them to sing! Everyone who was strong enough stood around the room, crowded around the bed. Maria sat on the edge, bending over her little girl. Mr Taylor led in a hymn and one by one the tired voices joined in. Another. And another. Gracie's breathing rattled and wheezed in the background. On and on they sang. Jeff noticed it was getting dusk. Still another hymn. Most of them Jeff knew. Others must have been hymns they sang in England, he guessed. He sang along as well as he could.

Finally, the room was quieter. He was aware of that but it took a minute to register what had happened. The sound of noisy breathing had stopped. There was a hush. Jeff glanced at Gracie's face. It was so relaxed now. Peaceful. At first he thought she was just asleep but then he realized the reason she looked so peaceful. She was in heaven.

Somewhere from the group a sob broke the silence. Now everyone was crying openly; even Tsiu had tears streaming down his shiny brown cheeks. Jeff swallowed quickly. He didn't want the tears to start. He tightened and relaxed the muscles in his legs and stole a quick glance at the faces around him.

Maria had her face on Gracie's, forehead to forehead. Her tears wet the little girl's still face and ran silently onto the sheets. Hudson walked around the bed and knelt beside her now, his arm around both Maria and Grace. His shoulders shook quietly and he kept running his hands through Gracie's once-long curls.

There was no screaming, no anger, no wailing, only a quiet sadness and, Jeff thought, a sort of mournful peace. Like it was too bad, but at the same time it was all right. Was that possible? Could something this bad be acceptable? One by one everyone tiptoed from the room, leaving Hudson and Maria alone with Gracie for the last time.

Mr Taylor emerged from the room a while later. "We'll go back to Hangzhou at once, of course," he said. "But we must be careful not to let anyone know the reason for our sudden departure. If the temple priests and other residents or tourists know a death has taken place, they could cause a great commotion and demand sacrifices. They always want to appease the spirits of the dead." Jeff understood what that meant. Of course the Christians would refuse to offer sacrifices to spirits, so that would make the local people really angry. No telling what might result. Yes, they would have to leave quietly and inconspicuously. Even at a time like this Mr Taylor would be the one to care about such details.

Jeff watched as the men piled blankets and pillows in the small tin bathtub which they always took with them. Then with great care, Gracie's body was laid on top of the pillows, and more pillows and blankets were piled on top of her. Now it looked like just an ordinary tub full of bedding, a common sight for Chinese travelers.

The moon was shining full as they started down the hillside. Mr Williamson and Mr Taylor carried the tub between them, Mrs Taylor and the children came next, and everyone else followed single file down the path to the water's edge. The boats were waiting. As casually as he dared, Mr Williamson took the tub on one shoulder and carried it aboard. Jeff thought it would be better if they were talking normally but he, like everyone else, didn't seem to have anything to say. Five hours later, the solemn procession walked through the gate of New Lane.

Now they could proceed with plans for a funeral. Grace's body was placed lovingly inside the coffin. Maria picked a rose from the garden and placed it in Gracie's hands, curling the fingers around it. Her little girl looked beautiful as always.

One of the Chinese Christians who had been especially friendly with Grace was a skilled painter and decorator, and he volunteered to work on the coffin. For three weeks he lacquered and waxed and polished it till it shone like a mirror. It was ready. In the garden where Gracie used to play, a Chinese style grave was built above ground, like a little house. The coffin was placed inside and, after a simple service on the spot, the grave was sealed.

Tsiu came over and stood beside Jeff after the crowd had gone quietly back to the house. "She gone, little Gracie."

"Yeah."

"Spirit already gone to be with Jesus. Now body put away."

Jeff nodded. He needed time to think. So much was taking place every day. So much activity, yet so much sadness too. It wasn't like on TV. It was different when you were right there and it was somebody you knew.

Later that evening Herbert sat down beside Jeff under a shady tree in the rock garden. He wiggled over till his body was touching Jeff as they sat side by side. "You were right, Jeff," he said cheerfully. "I did get better. I didn't go to see Jesus yet."

Jeff forced some enthusiasm into his voice. "I told you so. I knew you'd make it. Feeling better these days?"

"Yes. But Mama says I'm still not eating enough. But I miss Gracie. Now I can't play with her or get her to help me with my school work."

"I know," Jeff nodded. "I miss her too."

"I prayed that God would make her better, but He didn't."

"No."

"He hears us pray. Why doesn't He give us what we ask for — especially something good like Gracie getting better?"

Jeff knew he would have to say something. Bertie wasn't the kind of kid you could ignore. But what could he say? If God didn't answer prayer for people like this who could expect answers? And why a child, a little girl like Gracie? Why not somebody older maybe, or somebody wicked, or somebody who deserved to die — why Gracie? And if Mr Taylor was right in what he always emphasized about trusting God and expecting God to give them everything they needed, why didn't He give Gracie good health? Or for that matter, why didn't He give them better living conditions? Or make the people accept the missionaries instead of trying to get rid of them? Or protect Tsiu when he was preaching?

Does Mr Taylor ever ask these kind of questions? wondered Jeff. If he did he didn't say so, at least not in Jeff's hearing. Still, Jeff noticed even Taylor's usual hopefulness that kept all the rest of them going was more subdued these days. Like something had been taken away and would never be filled, even though everything seemed the same on the outside.

During the next days Jeff found Bertie tagging along with him more and more often. He could understand that. But he didn't know if he was much help to the little boy, really. He had a lot of things still to settle for himself.

It was nearly a week later when Hudson Taylor put his arm around Jeff's shoulder. "Let's go for a walk. I've done all the medicine I can do for today." They passed through the city gate and strolled up a path they had taken often before. At Jeff's feet a grasshopper jumped to safety. "Gracie used to love to come up here. She loved that big tree."

Jeff nodded. They said no more for a few moments. The fragrance of honeysuckle blooms had attracted a swarm of bees whose steady buzz broke the silence. When Mr Taylor spoke again, his voice was soft. "This has been hard on you, I know."

Hard on me? Jeff thought. *What about you and Maria?* But that was just like Mr Taylor, always thinking more about everyone else's feelings than his own. "Yeah," he answered slowly. "I really liked Gracie. I guess I just don't see ..."

"Why did God let her die, is that what you mean? Why, when we all prayed for her, didn't He answer prayer." He said it more to himself than to Jeff, almost like he'd forgotten Jeff was there. "Sometimes I wonder why God does what He does, why He allows things like this. Sometimes

I wonder if I was wrong to think He called us out here, when it touches my children ..."

They stood overlooking the city clustered below them. Normally Mr Taylor would be gathering species of butterflies or trying to take a picture with his primitive camera. Now he just stared ahead and spoke hesitantly. It was as if his thoughts were forcing themselves out and Jeff listened, speechless. So even Mr Taylor had questions about things like this.

Hudson held both his hands over his mouth and rubbed them back and forth across his chin. His eyes filled with sudden tears. "No, I can't say that. God brought us here, I have to remind myself of that." He brought an immaculately white handkerchief from his pocket and wiped his nose. "If I can't understand why He does what He does, it's my understanding that's at fault, not His actions." He looked at Jeff again and said, almost in a whisper, "Let's think of it this way. Gracie's much better off now, isn't she? I wouldn't want her to be sick like that any longer. She's happy and well forever — how can I object to that?" Jeff could only nod.

The sound of farmers plodding home for the night reminded them what time it was. "We'd better head back. Maria will be wanting us for supper."

"By the way," Hudson said, his voice controlled again, "You've been a big help to us and we appreciate it, but you need a break. Why don't you go with Duncan up river to Nanjing."

Jeff jumped at the chance. It would be good to see some other city and besides, he always liked to be with George Duncan. The Chinese seemed to love the big Scottish mason as much as the missionaries did.

"Thanks. I'd be glad to."

"He leaves at dawn tomorrow so you'd better go get your things together."

As they glided smoothly up the Grand Canal the first day of their trip, Jeff relaxed with the feeling of the warm sun on his back and the rhythmic splashing of oars in the water. The boat was a flat bottomed junk with bamboo matting arched above it for a partial roof. Duncan leaned his bulky frame against the side of the boat and began to talk.

"Nanjing has been a big city for a long time," he told Jeff. "In fact it was the capital of the Ming dynasty, full of palaces. You know, Jeffrey, when Jesus Christ gave the command, 'Go into all the world and preach the gospel to every creature', Nanjing was already an important city. In Jesus' day! Yet how many people have been born, lived and died within the city without having ever heard that He came."

Jeff was silent. When you put it like that, it made it seem a whole lot more important for somebody to go and tell them.

Rivers and canals took the place of roads in this area, except for occasional narrow tracks paved with granite slabs. Mountains and valleys stretched off into distant mists. Part way up river they had to change to a smaller boat, better able to navigate the rapids and white-water.

Nanjing was picturesque. No doubt about that. But not very welcoming. No one would risk renting a room to a "foreign devil." They were afraid of the consequences they had been warned of.

Duncan was not perturbed. "Never mind. We'll sleep here on the boat until we can get something," he said cheerfully. "God will provide for us eventually." There was that answer again.

By day, Jeff trailed along behind Duncan as he walked the streets, giving out tracts and books and finding people who were willing to listen to the gospel. Jeff guessed Duncan's knowledge of the Chinese language wasn't as good as Mr Taylor's — somehow the accent didn't sound quite as authentic as when it rolled off Mr Taylor's or Maria's lips. But the highlander didn't seem to mind. Over and over again he gathered eager audiences and preached. Jeff was ready to quit long before Duncan ran out of enthusiasm.

Always they kept searching for a place to rent; always they were turned down.

"Here's a fellow we haven't asked," Duncan said one day, as they approached an old temple priest. "Would you know of any place we could rent for me to live?" he asked in his best Chinese.

Jeff didn't understand all the conversation that followed, but in a minute or two they set off after the man down a cobblestone street lined with buildings, to a wall with an archway under it. On top of the wall was a pagoda-like tower, three stories high. Each section was topped with shiny tile roofs with the tips turned gracefully upwards.

"He says this is the drum tower," Duncan explained.

"What on earth is that?"

"The tower where the announcer stands to beat the hours of the night and to give the alarm if there's a fire."

"Oh, brother! Like living in a firehall!"

But Duncan was not worried. It was a place to sleep. Soon he and Jeff had spread their straw mats and made themselves at home.

Sleep that night was not easy. Rats scurried across the floor and anything on it — including the sleepers. Every hour a heavy gong vibrated the floor under them. And when there was a town emergency or announcement, a mallet beaten rapidly on a round metal drum left Jeff's ears ringing. "I think that thing even makes the rats deaf," he said to Duncan.

"But look at it this way," Jeff joked with Duncan one night. "I don't know anyone who has ever occupied a hotel with such unique architectural characteristics. At least it's — well, original."

NINE
CPR Comes in Handy

"Don't you go to school, Jeffrey?" Bertie asked one day as he finished his day's assignments. The worst of the oppressive heat was over and everyone at New Lane seemed to be feeling healthier.

"Sure, I go to school. I'm in high school. I mean I'm going into ninth grade. That is, I would be if I were at home." Suddenly Jeff realized that in all the activities of the past months he had almost forgotten about trying to go home. Just for an instant a thought flicked through his mind, a thought of Northside High and all the things he was missing. Things like Mrs Reed's Spanish class and Mr Howard's Chemistry. And long, noisy bus rides and lunch in a brown bag ... he wasn't exactly sorry to be missing out on it. At least this was more exciting, and maybe even more useful, even though it would be awfully hard to explain!

Bertie continued, "I can't imagine going to a real school with a lot of other boys. I've always just had Mama and Miss Emily to teach me. And I'm the only one in my class."

Jeff grinned at him. "Then you must be the smartest. At least you always know who's going to get the best marks in exams." He was hoping to make Bertie feel better but actually he thought it would be pretty bad doing your schooling at home. Boring probably, and lonely.

"Miss Emily's a very good teacher," Bertie insisted. "I like to listen to her read. And you should hear her tell stories!"

Just then a movement at the gate caught Jeff's eye. It was the blue coat of his squint-eyed, skinny observer. This time the boy seemed to be bolder, just standing outside the gate, waiting for it to open. He didn't run away when he saw Jeff looking at him.

"That kid! He's not afraid of us any more. Not since that night we treated the opium addict. Just stands and stares now. I wish he'd go away once and for all."

"What kid?" Herbert asked.

"That one that's standing over there. See? He's here morning, noon and night. Just stares at me and follows me or your Dad around, watching everything we do. I'm surprised you haven't noticed him."

"Oh, you mustn't mind him, Jeffrey. Mama says they just watch us because they've never seen foreigners before and they have to see how we live. They're afraid of us, you know. So if they watch us long enough they might realize we're quite safe and not be afraid anymore. Then they'll come to hear Papa or Mr Tsiu preach about Jesus."

"Yeah, I know. That sounds great, and I guess I'm too sensitive, but I don't like somebody watching me all the time. Besides, he doesn't seem any closer to believing in Jesus now than he was weeks ago, even with all his watching. It bugs me to have him always around."

"Don't worry, I'll talk to him."

Jeff watched as Bertie walked over to the fence and began to talk to the boy. Quietly and politely — Jeff could see him smiling — he carried on a conversation for a few minutes. Then the boy turned and walked away and Bertie came back to Jeff.

"He says his name is Wu Liang and he just wants to see the big boy with light skin and round eyes. He's fascinated by you — you're about his own age but so different. I guess he's never seen such a funny looking thing before." Bertie giggled. "He was very polite really."

"Yeah, I'm sure I'm funny looking to him. I'd

be funny to Greg and Mom and Dad too if they saw me now in these clothes. But how did you get him to go away?"

"I just told him we were dull and boring to watch and weren't going to do anything but sit and talk, and he might like to go and play or go to the lake for some fish instead. Then he said if he caught some fish he would bring us back one for our dinner and I said that was a good idea. So that's where he's gone. See? Easy."

"Good for you! I don't care about his fish, but it was a good way to get rid of him for a while at any rate."

It wasn't more than an hour later when Jeff heard a commotion at the gate. Over the shouting and hurrying footsteps, a man's voice was calling for Mr Taylor. Tsiu opened the gate and in rushed a crowd. In the middle of it was a man with a body draped limply over his shoulder. Jeff could just see an unmoving form as the man struggled under the dead weight and the crowd pushed and jostled around them. A little trail of water dripped behind them as they moved.

Tsiu translated quickly as the man shouted. "He fell in lake and drowned."

Jenny Faulding came running out at the sound of the crowd. "Oh dear, what a time for an emergency," she said, "with Mr Taylor and Maria both away for the day. We'll have to do what we can."

"Take him to the treatment room," she instructed Tsiu. "Have them put him on the table. And see if you can get the rest of the crowd to clear out so we can work."

Tsiu took charge then as they disappeared into the clinic. Jeff felt his pulse racing and his mouth dry up. Drowned! He knew that if it were possible to revive a drowning victim at all, it had to be done quickly.

"There's not much one can do really," Miss Faulding said quietly to him.

"We can try CPR."

"I beg your pardon?"

There was no time to explain. "I think I know what to do. Come and help me." He raced toward the chapel and into the treatment room, Miss Faulding close behind him. There was nobody else to do it. He would have to do the best he could. If only he could remember the details. He had learned life-saving techniques in a Red Cross course last year when he took swimming lessons, but he'd never actually used them. "God, help me," he said under his breath. "It's the only chance."

He pushed through the group crowding around the table. Then he saw the victim — a skinny boy about his own age, clad in a dripping blue jacket, his face covered with pock marks. Even with his hair soaking wet and his face the shade of paper, he was recognizable. It was Wu Liang! The boy had gone fishing and must have fallen

in.   Jeff had been   glad to get rid of him, but
suddenly he felt guilty for having wished him gone.

There was no time for regrets now. He had
to remember what to do.   A ... B ... C ... A
was for airway. Establish an airway.   Airway, that
was the first thing. He flipped the boy onto his
back, placed his hands in position, one behind
his neck and one on his forehead. He gave a
push on the forehead, tipping the head back and
raising the chin so the tongue wouldn't block the
throat.

A ... B. B was breathing. That was the next
thing. Obviously the victim wasn't breathing. He'd
have to do mouth to mouth resuscitation. He
hesitated. Mouth to mouth ... on somebody like
this? It was one thing on a plastic dummy in
class, but ... this guy? Yuck! How could he put
his mouth over this guy's mouth? Goodness knows
what germs he might have, probably even TB.
Besides, dirty foam now oozed from around the
victim's lips and dirty water trickled slowly from
one corner of his mouth. He forced himself not
to think about it. "God ... help!" he prayed instantly.
There was no time to lose. He pinched off the
nose, put his head down to the boy's face and
without giving himself a chance to reconsider,
covered the boy's mouth with his own.

Breathe four times, he remembered. He puffed
four big breaths into the boy's lungs, pausing in
between only to suck in more air. He had to

work quickly. Still no breathing. He ran his fingers over the boy's skinny neck, feeling for a pulse at the carotid artery. None. He moved his fingers again; maybe he wasn't feeling in the right spot. No, he was sure; there was no pulse.

C ... that was the next thing, circulation ... had to get the circulation going. Find the breastbone, position the hands, one over the other, elbows locked, press. One — one thousand — one — two thousand — one — three thousand — one — four thousand — one — five thousand. Down and up he went. Press down on the "one", release on the "one thousand" and so on. Up and down. He gave two more quick breaths into the boy's mouth. The stench almost made him sick. Mustn't think about it. Back to work. External cardiac stimulation ... he could hear his instructor's voice clearly now, "It takes 80 to 100 pounds of pressure to press that sternum down enough to stimulate circulation. Press ..."

Push, count, release. Push, count, release. He must establish a rhythm. Down, one thousand, up, two thousand, down ... Over and over.

He did a frantic mental search for anything he might have forgotten. Clear airway. Establish breathing. He must keep on. "Once CPR begins it cannot be interrupted for more than five seconds," he remembered the teacher stressing. Thank goodness he had taken that course even though he didn't want to bother with it at the time.

Miss Faulding stood beside him watching, and probably praying, Jeff decided. Only a couple of people remained inside. The rest of the crowd had dispersed at Tsiu's instructions. They watched with anxious faces as Jeff carried on his rhythmical motions. "Come on, come on, breathe," he pleaded out loud. He knew what could happen if the boy didn't respond. The foreigners' medicine would have failed and the reputation of the missionaries and all they represented would be at stake. The people were already suspicious enough; it wouldn't take much to make them turn nasty. He hoped they'd understand that he was doing all he could.

His arms began to ache and his fingers were cramping, but he kept on. Just then the boy gasped and choked. Jeff kept up his work. Suddenly a gush of water came from the boy's mouth and in the next second his chest rose with inrushing air. Up and down. Up and down. As Jeff carried on, the boy's chest rose and fell, stronger and stronger now, till he was breathing on his own. Jeff remembered the instructor's voice, "Don't stop at the first breath. Maintain your resuscitation until breathing is firmly established." He watched the boy's face. Color gradually crept into the pockmarked cheeks and the eyelids began to flutter.

Excited voices began to jabber all at once and Tsiu nodded, smiling. "He is alive," he said, grinning. Pride showed on his face. "I told them he would live."

Jeff pulled his hands away as the boy opened his eyes. "How did you know he would? I must admit I wasn't so sure!"

"I pray," Tsiu answered.

Jeff nodded. "Yeah, me too," he said softly. "Me too."

The boy struggled to a sitting position and looked around a little dazedly. His eyes met Jeff's. A look of fear came to his eyes and then, slowly, a shy smile formed on his lips and quickly spread across his face in a big grin. The fear had vanished. He reached out his hand to Jeff, saying something. Jeff smiled, grabbed his hand and shook it.

"He say, thank you," Tsiu told him. "He like you very much now."

"I guess so! He'd be dead otherwise!" Jeff laughed. Suddenly he felt relief sweep all over him. His arms suddenly turned to jelly and he realized how tired he was from his efforts. But he had succeeded. He looked at Wu Liang's smiling face, then he sank down to the floor, exhausted. "You can tell him I like him too and I'm glad he's all right."

The daily routine soon took over again. More and more people were now living under the same roof and No 1, New Lane was more of a hotel than a family home. For one thing new workers had arrived to help the China Inland Mission and more were due soon. One of those was to be

Catherine Brown, who was coming out from Scotland to marry George Duncan.

"What's she like?" Jeff asked his friend one day. "Your fiancée. Tell me about her."

The rugged highlander's solid face broke into a grin and a twinkle came to his eyes. "A bonnie lass, she is. Twenty-three years old. Beautiful. She'll do fine anywhere — even in a station up-country away from Shanghai. She'll not be put off by difficulties. Takes a special kind of lady for the life I have to offer, y'know."

"That's for sure! One that's able to sleep in a bell tower with rats running over her and gongs ringing in her ears all night long!"

They both laughed. "Aye, it was quite a place, wasn't it," Duncan admitted. "But you've not seen my current place. I've got a fine one now, so I have. Three real rooms on a second floor. Hopefully in a short while the landlord will let me rent the bottom half too, and then we'll have the whole building and even have room to make a little chapel out of the downstairs. It's not a bad place to take a lady — if she's the right kind of lady. And Catherine's special. Yes indeed."

The Hangzhou house was full. With the printing press now occupying one room, and the Taylors, Rudlands, Jenny Faulding, Emily Blatchley and the McCarthys all living there, and Catherine still to come, Mr Taylor felt it was time for the group to spread out.

"Too many of us in one place," he said. "Not only is it crowded for us, but it arouses too much suspicion among the Chinese. More likely to draw attention to ourselves and stir up trouble. Besides, there are fifty Christians now in the church here, and some of them are quite good leaders; they don't need us. If we mean to spread out to other cities now's the time."

The group seemed to agree. "My wife and I could stay here and keep the clinic going," Dr McCarthy offered. "We don't know the language very well yet, but if someone more experienced were to stay with us ... like Jenny Faulding, for instance ..."

"Of course," Taylor agreed delightedly. "That'll be fine. I'd like to see Jenny carry on her ministry here anyway — she's so well accepted by everyone in this area. What d'you say, Jenny?"

"There's no place I'd rather be than right here," Jenny agreed. "I'll miss all of you when you go, of course. But I agree, it's a good chance to reach another area, and that's what we came for. Where will you go?"

"Yangzhou. The big city further north on the Grand Canal — the city Marco Polo once governed. Do you realize Yangzhou has a population of 360,000 and no Christian witness at all! If we can find a house to rent there we'll live in Yangzhou."

TEN

We're going to be killed!

The rambling house which they were finally able to rent in Yangzhou was soon full too. The Rudlands were to set up residence in the nearby city of Zhenjiang, but when they arrived with two boat-loads of belongings, including the printing press, no house was available, so they had to move in with the rest of the Yangzhou crowd. Besides the Taylors and Emily Blatchley there were other missionaries and children, plus twelve or thirteen Chinese helpers. And always, the visitors. Chinese came and went freely, roaming all over the property until Miss Blatchley made a regulation that they could not go upstairs to the bedrooms. Even so, there seemed to be no end to the stream of visitors, especially women, who came and went. They were all friendly, fortunately, and some even seemed interested in the gospel.

"Negotiations may be a bit slow when it comes to renting the house in Zhenjiang," Taylor said one afternoon. "No one's willing to rent to a foreigner." He sank down on the couch with a groan.

"You're sick, aren't you?" Maria said to him. "You should really stay in bed a few days till you feel better. You'll find a place to rent eventually. It just takes time."

"I know, I know. I'm glad we've got this place anyway."

Maria reassured him as she poured a cup of tea for them both. "At least it's a start. We've moved away from the coast. From here we can begin to reach out north and west as more workers join us."

"I hope that's soon. There's a lot of territory out there and we've barely touched it."

"Don't worry. It won't be long before we have workers in every province as God allows us to."

"I know, I get impatient sometimes. Especially at times like this when I get sick and feel so ... so useless. Like I'm wasting time. I need to keep reminding myself that it's God work we're doing. And God's work, done in God's way ..."

"... will never lack God's supply," Maria finished. "I've heard you say it so often, Hudson." She laughed and touched his hand. "That could almost be our motto, couldn't it. And if ever we needed God's supply it's now — His supply of wisdom that is, and a good portion of courage too. I'm afraid the feelings against us ... Who's that knocking?"

The knock came again. Louder this time, on the door that led to the street. Jeff hurried to open it. They weren't expecting anyone else since the house was already full. Who could it be? To his delight, there stood the burly form of the Scotsman, George Duncan.

"I thought you were on your way to Shanghai to meet your girlfriend," Jeff said, closing the door behind him.

"I was but John McCarthy's going to wait there for her and escort her back up, since the ship's been delayed. Thought I'd call in here a wee while and see how everyone is. Where's Mr Taylor? I've some news for him."

Jeff led the way to where Mr Taylor was resting on the couch. No sooner had they moved in than all the children and some of the servants came down with measles. Now Mr Taylor himself had been sick several days. It seemed one crisis just followed another. And from the look of Duncan's face there was more bad news to come.

"There's trouble brewing," Duncan said briskly. "As I came through the city just now I saw huge posters all over the city walls. I hate to tell you, but they were worse than the handbills they printed earlier. These are directed against missionaries, specifically. Some are over three feet long, blazoned all over the town, saying things like, 'Down with the Brigands of the Religion of Jesus'."

Mr Taylor sighed. "I know. There's been trouble in several quarters lately; I'm not surprised it's broken out here. We've been accused of gouging out people's eyes, eating children, even doing surgery to remove people's organs so we can sell them, if you please."

He got up slowly and began to walk around the room. "I had a letter today, anonymous of course, warning us to expect a riot tomorrow. Whether it's true or not, one never knows, but I fear we may be in for it."

Duncan was not one to waste time speculating. "Let's get to work. You rest, sir. This young man'll help me, won't you?" he said, looking at Jeff with a smile that belied the tension in the room. "We'll barricade the doors. Here, take this."

Jeff and George Duncan set to work, finding as many heavy pieces of furniture as possible. Some bricks in the courtyard came in handy for repairing part of a wall and closing another opening.

"Here, help me drag this heavy trunk out. It'll be a good barricade for that door."

Everyone volunteered whatever heavy furniture he had. Jeff brought two chairs from the chapel to place in front of the doorway leading from the street into a long hallway.

"They won't be heavy enough by themselves,

but if we sit on them it'll add weight," he told Duncan.

"Aye, I reckon I'll add a few pounds to give the rioters a bit of difficulty pushing their way in," Duncan laughed softly. Jeff appreciated his quiet humor at a time like this. He felt safer with Duncan around. Nevertheless he was glad that Mr Taylor had just hired two deputy sheriffs as doorkeepers a few days before. They could at least lend an air of authority to the defense efforts.

They were none too soon. No sooner had they finished with their preparations than a barrage of stones crashed against an upstairs window. Now someone was pounding the outer wall. Not just someone — a mob. It sounded like a crowd armed with clubs. The noise was getting worse. From the voices there must have been hundreds of people crowding at the door. So far no one had broken in, but the "chair-sitters" guarding the door wouldn't be able to keep out intruders much longer.

"Boy, am I glad you stayed to help," Jeff whispered to Duncan as they took their turn lending ballast to the chair barricade. "I'm sorry you won't be there to meet Catherine when she comes in, but I'm sure glad you're here. Mr Taylor isn't well enough to do much by himself and Mr Rudland and Mr Reid have their hands full too. I don't know what we'd do without you."

"Aach, 'tis nothing. I'm glad to help. With Catherine's ship being a couple of months late, it'll give me something to occupy my mind while I wait for her. By the way, we'll be getting married in September, you know. You must come to the wedding."

Just then Tsiu came back from the market with disturbing news. Jeff depended on Duncan for an interpretation. From the way everyone was buzzing he knew it was something worth hearing. "A new handbill circulated in town," Duncan explained. "Says that on Tuesday, that's examination day for the school graduates, when they all gather in Yangzhou, they'll form a mob of students and local citizens and assemble on the town square for a wee demonstration."

"What are they going to do?" Jeff asked, panic sneaking into his voice in spite of himself. He wished he could feel as calm as Duncan sounded.

"They'll be marchin' here to burn down the house, so they say. Hopin' to destroy everyone in it. They're meanin' business, this time."

Jeff choked and stared at the calm, quiet man who was telling him this.

"You mean we're all going to be killed. That's it. That's the bottom line, isn't it?" Jeff felt his mouth suddenly go dry as dust.

"What quaint expressions you have! 'Bottom line'. But I understand." He chuckled. "Yes, they want us to think so. But ... and here's a big but ... the day hasn't come yet. We don't know what will happen. They could well change their mind. And above all," he put his hands on Jeff's shoulders and looked straight into his eyes, "don't forget, lad, we are not without resources." He narrowed one eye in a slow wink. "We have the God of Heaven for our help, you know."

Jeff shrugged and turned his eyes away. George Duncan's soft brogue had a reassuring tone but Jeff wasn't so easily convinced. Of course God could help, but still, it'd sure be nice to see some visible evidence that He was doing something about it right now.

Tuesday morning was grey and chilly. Would the students march on the house and burn it down? The household went about their business as usual. Morning prayers were longer and more intense but no one seemed unduly alarmed. Jeff was scared stiff. *I don't want to be anywhere near here, not even in this century, and here I am — going to be surrounded and killed by a mob in nineteenth century China. This can't be happening. There's got to be a way out of this.*

But there didn't seem to be. Never mind hoping Uncle Zeke would figure out a way to get him back. First he had to live through the crisis at hand, and concentrate on surviving.

As he took his place at the outside door, he put his eye to the crack in the wall. What he

saw looked like a bizarre parade. Students, peas-
ants, wealthy landlords, hundreds of local citizens,
were marching towards the mission compound.
Some were clanging cymbals, students yelled
slogans and chanted. The earth vibrated with the
steady drum of feet, coming, coming, closer and
closer.

Jeff couldn't stop his teeth from chattering.

"Are you afraid, Jeff?" He jumped and turned
around. It was Mr Taylor, standing beside him.
Jeff thought he looked very tired but he was smiling.
Jeff was a bit ashamed to admit the terror he
felt. He nodded and Mr Taylor put an arm around
him, taming his shivering somewhat.

"Let me have a peek out your little spy-hole
here. Ah, yes, they're coming as they said. Well,
now's the time to trust the great power of our
God."

How can he say that, Jeff wondered. *He acts
like nothing's wrong. Or like God is just going
to step in and protect us all. How do we know
He will?* The crowd was getting louder now. Stones
and sticks were hitting the windows and throughout
the crowd well-dressed men, obviously influential,
were moving around talking and agitating the mob,
trying to stir up trouble. The dark sky only seemed
to add gloom to the terror.

Jeff watched, unable to take his eyes off the
scene. "We've done all we can do," Mr Taylor
was saying. "We can only trust God now. Anyway,

look at that sky. A good rain now will do more for us than a whole army of soldiers." As he spoke, a loud clap of thunder rumbled over the crowd. Still the agitators tried to get action going. Another clap of thunder and now lightning with it. Somewhere upstairs a shutter banged. Wind must be getting strong. Jeff could hear the trees bending and whistling in the courtyard just beside the wall. The crowd grew restless, louder.

Suddenly a torrent of rain burst onto the scene. Grey sheets of water poured from the sky like it had never rained before. Jeff turned to Mr Taylor and a grin came to his face. He put his eye to the hole again and the grin widened. He could hardly believe it. The crowd was dispersing. All of them had turned around and were running for shelter. No use setting fire to anything in weather like this. Except for the deafening roar of rain on the roof, all was quiet.

"D'ye hear that?" Duncan said. "Only storm. No yelling, no banging. They've gone and left us alone, praise the Lord." The little group breathed a sigh of relief.

There was that rain again, thought Jeff. *Just when we needed it.* The rain that he used to complain about ... As the rain continued, Jeff had to admit that it did look as if God had done something for them after all.

As the days passed with no return of the mob, George Duncan took advantage of the lull in the violence to leave for some business in a neighboring town. The head count now at the Yangzhou house was four men, five women and four children among the missionaries, plus nineteen Chinese colleagues, printers and servants. The printing press and many other things were stored in rooms off the courtyard. And a courier had just brought three hundred dollars from Zhenjiang to help with the expenses of the overflowing household. To the townspeople, the mission compound was a treasure-house of wealth. If the rioters were to strike now, it would certainly be worth their while. Jeff didn't like the thought.

When Duncan returned Saturday night, he looked worried. Barring the door tightly behind him, he said urgently, "There's a great crowd out there. Worse than before — and angrier. They're saying we have eaten 24 children. There'll be no stoppin' them this time, I fear."

As the minutes passed, the mob grew and the noise became more threatening. A hail of stones pelted the windows, sending broken glass shattering everywhere. The constant chanting was punctuated by shouts and gongs. The hubbub almost drowned out Mr Taylor's voice as the group crowded together to pray. Jeff heard him say, "Lord, we are in your hands." Then he turned to give instructions.

Jeff and George Duncan pulled more stuff in front of doors, and the women and children were sent upstairs to the inner bedrooms. "Not as much danger of you being hit with flying debris or broken windows there," Mr Taylor said. "They've occupied the room at the front and the room at the back and both gates. You can't leave, you can only stay together in the middle rooms upstairs and hope to ride out the storm."

"There's thousands of people out there," Tsiu hissed. "Ten thousand at least."

"We're going to have to make a run for it and go across town to the Prefect to get help," Mr Taylor said. "With all the women and children upstairs, we'll have to leave Rudland and Jeff here, and you come with me, Duncan."

"Right, sir. But the mob is closing in on both gates and every exit. How will we get through?"

"We'll go through the kitchen into the neighbor's house, and from there I know a back way — a field we can cut through without being seen. I hope."

They took one last look at the fortifications, such as they were. "You'll be all right here then, won't you," George Duncan said to Jeff. "Do the best you can, and we'll get help as quickly as possible. Surely the Prefect will be bound to send help rather than risk an international incident." He started to follow Mr Taylor to the kitchen, hesitated an instant and turned back. "Don't forget," he said softly, looking at Jeff's fearful face, "God is with us."

As quietly as possible they slipped out through a side passage. Jeff watched them go with the sudden sickening realization that he might never see them again. He saw Duncan bend low to duck into a doorway. If the highlander was afraid it didn't show.

It was only a few minutes before Jeff heard loud shouting from the mob.

"They see him," Tsiu interpreted. "They say, 'foreign devils escape'." That was it. A mob that size could catch the two men in an instant, and undoubtedly they intended to kill them.

Jeff could hear Mrs Taylor upstairs talking gently to Herbert and the other children. "God will look after Papa. And us as well." *She must have heard the crowd, too,* Jeff thought. *She knows the crowd is out for their blood. How can she go on saying God is going to look after them?*

He leaned harder against the wall. They would be really angry now. The wall built up to bar the side entrance was now down and the mob was pushing further and further inside the house. Rudland and Mr Reid held them off as long as they could at their posts and Jeff at his, but little by little the doors were giving way.

"Still, they haven't yet reached the stairway, so the folks upstairs are safe," Rudland whispered to Jeff. "Our only chance, when we can't hold out any longer, is to climb the ladder to the upstairs and pull the trap door shut. That'll give us one last stronghold. Maybe that way we can make it till help comes." He was exhausted. Mud splattered his clothes, and his face and arms were bruised and cut. Jeff knew the man had been hit with bricks and sticks hurled from the gathering mob.

"Go on up and have a rest for a few minutes. Mr Reid and I'll manage here," Jeff said, pushing him towards the stairway. "Just don't close the trap door and cut us off." The man nodded. He was hardly able to crawl up the stairs. Mr Reid was alone at his post now and the wall beside him was buckling under the mob. Jeff was almost giving way too. There was nothing more he could do. The rioters were chanting and yelling. Jeff hoped desperately that Mr Taylor and Duncan had made it to the prefecture to get help. But he knew there was little hope of that. After all, the rioters had seen them and would have been after them instantly. They were probably dead by now ... and there was no help coming!

The door cracked and Jeff jumped as a hand came through, grabbing his shirt. He pulled away and ran for the stairs. Then he saw what was happening. Through the crack in the door seeped a puff of smoke. He could see a torch glowing outside and suddenly, on his right, a blaze shot into the air.

"Fire!" he yelled. "Fire!" Jeff raced for the ladder to the upper floor, shouting to Mr Reid, "Help!

They're setting the house on fire!"

Mr Reid reached out and grabbed his shirt. "Get down! Get everyone out of here." He shouted, "Mrs Taylor, come down. They've set the place on fire. We can't hold them off any longer."

ELEVEN

"These people do not murder children"

Maria's calm, tightly controlled voice answered, "We can't get out except through the windows. We'll go onto the roof."

Jeff ran upstairs to help. "Throw down all pillows," Maria ordered. "We can jump onto them." Someone was stripping sheets from the beds, and he tied two together to make a sheet-rope. Maria handed the little children out the window onto the roof. The heat was getting worse now. Smoke billowed up from below.

"Stay there," Jeff said to Bertie who was standing, shaking and bewildered, on the steep roof. "Stand back from the edge and stay put till I tell you to jump. I'll go down first and catch you."

He stepped over the roof's edge, grabbed the

sheet and slid to the ground of the courtyard below. Buildings all around it were burning now, flames leaping high into the night sky. By their light he could see a pile of rubbish had been heaped up along the wall under the second floor balcony and set on fire. It blazed and darted, flames leaping almost to the roof where Maria and Mrs Rudland stood with the children.

Maria dropped Samuel down to Mr Reid's waiting arms. Jeff stood below Herbert. "Jump, Bertie. Jump. I'll catch you."

The little boy looked around at his mother. He was not crying but his eyes were wide with fear and confusion. "Go ahead, Bertie," Maria urged calmly. "Jump to Jeffrey. You'll be all right."

Bertie took a few steps to the edge of the roof, hesitated only a second then crouched down, knees bent, and flung himself off the roof. A tongue of flame lapped upwards just as he did so. Jeff opened his arms. "Come on, Bertie." He doubled as the child landed in his arms. It was all he could do to catch him but he set him gently on the ground and turned to catch Freddie who was right behind him.

Mr Reid quickly ushered the children away, warning them to silence, and Jeff saw them in the shadows as they entered the well-house across the yard. A minute later, a servant carrying baby Maria dashed out and ran frantically into the well-house behind them. They would be safe there for now.

Meanwhile Jeff saw men going in and out helping themselves to the things that were lying around, open to their view. One by one the other adults jumped onto the pillows and blankets they had thrown to the ground. Only Mr Rudland, Emily Blatchley and Mrs Taylor were left in the building.

Suddenly, a tall man with no shirt stepped out of an upstairs window in the darkness, grabbed Mr Rudland by the hair and threw him down on the tile roof. For a few seconds they scuffled, the assailant pushing Mr Rudland to the edge. Jeff saw Rudland grab for the window frame desperately but he couldn't reach it. He was slipping and clutching. Jeff watched helplessly from below. Then Miss Blatchley and Maria Taylor reached out the window together and grabbed Mr Rudland's coat, dragging him back towards them. Rudland struggled to his feet.

The assailant was angry. He picked up a brick, waved it over his head and took a step toward Mrs Taylor. Just as he was about to hit her Jeff heard her say something to him in Chinese. He cursed, threw down the brick and ran across the tiles, pulling the makeshift sheet rope down with him.

The escape rope was gone, the stairs were completely blocked by fire, and the courtyard under the roof edge was a sheet of flames. Jeff realized sickeningly that there was no way for Maria and

Miss Blatchley to get off the burning roof without jumping into the fire.

Mr Reid rushed over to the burning pile of debris. He reached for it and dragged it a few feet before the fire made him drop it. Immediately Jeff jumped over to help him. Twice more they darted in and pulled the fiery pile a few more feet. Jeff could smell the hair on his arms being singed. But they had cleared a small space for Miss Blatchley and Maria to land. They would have to jump, and there was no time to lose.

Mr Reid called Emily, "Jump here. I'll catch you. You too, Mrs Taylor, come ..."

Suddenly a brickbat came hurtling from the mob. It hit Mr Reid with full force right on his left eye. Jeff saw the man instinctively grab his head and fall, groaning, to the ground. But it was too late for Emily. She had already jumped. Now she landed with a hard thud right beside Jeff. He heard the bump of her skull hitting the stones. She lay flat on her back, her left arm flung against a pile of debris and broken glass. For a second she was motionless.

"Miss Blatchley, are you all right? Can you hear me?" Jeff shouted, bending over her.

She pulled herself up and attempted to get to her feet. "Ooh, my head is spinning. I'm very dizzy." She sunk back again. After two or three attempts, she pulled herself to her feet. "Yes, I think I'm all right." She brushed herself off.

"Oh, my arm! I've hurt my arm."

There was no time for Jeff to respond. Maria still had to jump. With Mr Reid injured, there was no one to catch her. Jeff determined to try to break her fall as best he could. She stepped boldly to the edge of the roof and flung herself towards the ground. Jeff stood under her, reaching for her as she fell. His arm slowed her fall somewhat but she landed on the ground with her right leg curled under her.

"Mrs Taylor, are you all right?" he asked as she gathered herself into a sitting position.

"No, I seem to have sprained my ankle. Or twisted it. Ooooh! I can't walk."

"Come on. We've got to get out of here. I'll help you," Jeff urged. Mr Rudland had jumped safely off the roof now and was gathering the children from the well-house. Mr Reid was conscious, but every move made him groan and stagger. Jeff could see he was close to fainting. But there was no time to lose. Even as they gathered themselves together, bricks were being hurled all around them. Some missed their target and cracked on the stones. One grazed Mr Rudland's arm.

"Hurry," Jeff yelled. "This way." He was supporting Maria, and little Herbert grabbed his other hand tightly as they made their way to the entrance. Suddenly another brick whizzed out of nowhere, catching Jeff just behind the ear. His head spun and he felt sick to his stomach.

He pulled his hand out of Bertie's clinging grasp and touched the left side of his head. Blood was trickling from somewhere, and his ear felt hot and sore. Still, it didn't hurt too much, and as the first reaction passed he felt less faint. It would have to wait. He grabbed Herbert's hand again and helped Maria limp on.

Mr Rudland, leading the party, stopped at the door by the chapel. "It's closed," he said. The wounded group shuffled to a stop. "Locked and barred." He looked around for another exit. "Quickly, back this way."

More bricks landed around them. Jeff felt himself beginning to float in and out of alertness. Mr Rudland said something but Jeff didn't hear it. He followed the group, making an effort to push one foot in front of the other, Maria leaning on one arm, Bertie clinging to the other. Move. They must keep moving.

"Here, this wall is down. We can climb over," Mr Rudland said. "Easy now." He helped first one and then the other as they struggled over the pile of bricks and out into the dark yard of a neighbour. It seemed extra dark after the flames they had just experienced.

This neighbor had always been friendly to them. It was their only chance of refuge. They poured into his house, limping, bleeding, half-dazed. Jeff followed woodenly, hardly aware of what was going on. They were herded into a dark room in th middle of the house and Jeff sank exhausted to the floor. The dejected party huddled close to one another. No one spoke. The noise of the mob grew louder and more fierce outside; the rioters were getting closer. They'd have to move to another room.

Quickly they gathered the children and sneaked across the hallway, following their host to a more hidden room. They must keep the children awake, Miss Blatchley said, in case they had to move again. Herbert and Freddie whimpered sleepily. Two or three times they moved, first one room then another. Together they huddled in the darkness, injured and shaken, hoping the rioters would be satisfied and leave them alone. Jeff's ear was swelling and the side of his head ached.

"Mama," Bertie said softly, "where will we sleep tonight? They have burned up our beds."

It seemed they had burned up more than that, Jeff thought. The whole house was going up in flames even as they sat there.

Maria looked at Bertie and ran her thin fingers through his blond hair. "I don't know, darling. Maybe we won't sleep in our own beds tonight. But God will find us some place to sleep."

Jeff knew Maria's main fear was not the beds, or the house full of stuff that had been burned. He knew she was wondering, as all of them were, what happened to Mr Taylor and George Duncan? Would they ever reach the Prefect's residence? They should have been back by now ...

Jeff faded off to a restless sleep, Bertie's head resting on his lap. Would help ever come?

He awoke to a familiar voice. He opened his eyes slowly and looked around. The disheveled group still huddled, trembling and scared, in the half-dark room. Then he saw Mr Taylor.

"I'm so glad to see you all safe! I feared they had burned the place down with you in it." He ran over to Maria and knelt down beside her. "Oh, what a relief to see you," he kept saying.

"We were afraid you had been seen and killed! Why did you take so long?" Maria asked.

"That's a long story. We got away from the mob by running through a field and coming to the Prefect's house a back way. But when we got there, the door was closed and the crowd was there before us. They almost killed us. We pounded on the gates, the mob screaming at our heels. I yelled the usual cry, 'Save life, save life'. A Chinese official is bound to open up when he hears that. But what really saved us was your friend." Hudson Taylor was looking at Jeff.

"What? Who are you talking about?" Jeff sat up now, suddenly wide awake.

"Look, let us get everyone out of here and back to our house again. I'll tell the rest of the story later."

"Isn't it burned to the ground?" one of the women asked.

"No, the neighbors intervened for us and helped put out the fires. It's a terrible mess, but it's still standing and the mob has gone. We might as well move back in. At least we'll be in our own place."

It was just past midnight. Slowly and stiffly the members of the bedraggled group limped across the yard to their house. Jeff dragged himself upstairs to the bedroom. The acrid stench of smoke hurt his nostrils. Shutters hung by one hinge, parts of the roof were gone, walls were broken down, doors had lost their hinges and trunks and boxes lay wide open. Everyone's belongings were scattered everywhere.

Jeff picked up what remained of the box of plates Mr Taylor had made to use in his camera. Around them lay shreds of photographs he had managed to take over the previous months, torn and scattered.

"Too bad they got your photography supplies."

Taylor shrugged. "I wasn't having much success with them anyway." He stooped down and sifted through a pile of rubble, what remained of his medical journals, a few pages torn from his Bible.

"I'm afraid they've taken everything of any value," Mr Taylor said. Jeff remembered all the money they had just received from Shanghai, which was supposed to last them for weeks. "With everything open like this ..."

Miss Blatchley came running down the hall,

interrupting him. "They didn't enter my room," she said, a tone of awe in her voice. "Look, the door was open. They could have gone in. But it's untouched." They followed her to her room.

She opened the drawer where the household money was kept. It had not been disturbed. She picked it up and fingered it slowly, letting the wonder of it sink in. Three hundred dollars. All there.

Mr Taylor said quietly, "Thank the Lord for that. All our most important papers ... and the money. All safe."

Jeff felt a cold chill running over him. In all the damage they did, they actually left the money! Only God could have possibly had a hand in that! He didn't stop the riot, but He had spared their lives and protected some of their possessions. God was with them in it after all.

Everyone fell exhausted into bed. He heard Bertie's high-pitched young voice saying to Maria, "Mama, we are in our own beds after all. You were right."

The morning dawned bright and warm. Jeff wondered what time it was. Had he slept till noon? He rubbed a hand over his ear. It still hurt but didn't seem to be serious. The blood had dried around it and his hair was sticky at that side but that would wash.

"I'd like to hear the rest of the story about

last night, sir," he said to Mr Taylor later.

"Ah, yes. It seems the boy who watched you for so long — Wu Liang — is on our side. When you saved his life you put all his suspicions to rest, no doubt, and won him over. He arrived in town sometime yesterday, not knowing anything was going on. He was on his way here to see us when he saw the mob, and heard enough of the shouting to know they meant to kill us.

"So, agile thing that he is, he was able to crawl away under the legs of the agitators without their paying any attention. He raced to the Prefect's ahead of us. When we got there the crowd was gathering strength — several thousand by that time — but the boy managed to squeeze through without arousing any suspicions and pushed his way in at the same time we did. Then he disappeared.

"Well, after we got inside the walls, we were taken to the secretary's office and had to wait almost an hour. We could hear the crowd yelling in the background and could imagine what they might be doing. The suspense was terrible. Anyway, when the Prefect finally came he began to question us. What did we really do with the babies? How many had we bought? Where were the bodies, etc. We could hardly stand to answer such nonsense, but God helped us keep cool and answer everything patiently.

"That's where Wu Liang came in. It turns out

the Prefect's second wife is his mother's sister. He visits his aunt from time to time, bringing her gifts from her parents and so on, so his presence in the compound didn't arouse any suspicion at all. Well, his aunt believed him when he said the foreigners had saved his life, so she sent for the Prefect, saying she had a message. He left us for a few minutes and when he came back he had the boy with him.

"I could see the poor boy was frightened. Very brave of him, really. He could certainly have been killed. The Prefect said, 'This boy says you saved his life.' I said nothing. Wu Liang kept insisting, 'These people do not murder children. I have seen with my own eyes.'

"Then he went on to tell how he had watched you, and all of us, for days and how we treated that man who took the opium overdose. And how you eventually saved his life when he nearly drowned. Of course I had nothing to do with that — I wasn't even home. I don't know how you knew ... Anyway he was very convincing and the Prefect's attitude seemed to change as he listened. Apparently he believed him, because then he said, 'Sit still and I'll go and see what can be done.'

"He was gone for a couple of hours. Wu Liang stayed with us. That's when we learned his story. All this time we were worried sick about you all. But finally he returned and said he had sent the rioters home, posted guards for our protection and had sedan chairs ready to bring us back. We still didn't know whether all of you might be dead. That's why we were so relieved to find everyone in the house next door."

"Whew! Sounds like you had as bad a time as we did! It was a pretty close call for all of us."

"We have a lot to be thankful for," Maria said.

Jeff nodded. His mind was full. Imagine that kid that had been such a pest turning out to be a hero! What if he hadn't been able to save the guy's life when he was in trouble? Or what if he had chased him out when he hung around, like he really wanted to do? Or what if ...

"Boy, I can really see how God was looking after us in this whole mess," he exclaimed. "I didn't think so before, but now I can see it." His mind whirled. "I didn't realize how tired a bit of excitement could make a person," he said, grinning. "I'm bushed. I could sleep for a week."

TWELVE
Everything under control

By the time they had eaten breakfast the crowd
was almost as thick as the night before, and from
the sound of it, just as wild. And this time no
one was well enough to put up much of a struggle.
Mr Rudland was unable to move. Maria and Miss
Blatchley both had injuries. Everyone was sore
and stiff, some worse than others.

Hudson Taylor decided to go and see the Prefect
again, and insist on official help. This time he
was unmolested. The Prefect must have given some
orders they all respected.

Jeff helped pick up what was left of everyone's
possessions. He was able to replace some of the
boards on the holes in the wall, and fix one of
the doors. But things were far from normal.

For the first time since the riot Jeff had a

few minutes to take note of himself. He had a zee-shaped cut about two inches long over his left ear, his hair was matted around it from blood, but the bleeding seemed to have stopped. His clothes were a mess. In fact, his wadded Chinese gown had burn holes all over the front. The left sleeve, grazed by the brick that hurt his head, was in tatters. A long streak of black soot marked the back.

"What a mess!" Jeff remarked to Maria as he assessed the situation.

"Yes, you definitely need a new jacket. Throw that one away. But I don't think we have any more that fit you and it'll be a few days before Miss Blatchley or I can get one made."

"Never mind. I'll change back into my own clothes in the meantime. Won't hurt for a few days." He pulled his teeshirt over his head. He'd forgotten how good the soft cotton felt against his skin.

About noon, Mr Taylor returned. This time the Prefect rode with him, and the crowd melted quietly away as they approached. Mr Taylor talked to the Prefect out in front of the house for a few minutes, and Jeff watched them go through the usual polite ritual of saying goodbye.

Things were under control now, he guessed. Mr Taylor's face looked sober and tired. *No wonder,* Jeff thought. *We all look pretty bad.* But as he talked, Taylor sounded calm. "We will have to leave temporarily while the Prefect restores order. But we will be back. We have his promise of protection." Then a smile spread over his face.

"Jeff, here's a friend to see you," he said, beckoning towards the door. In came the boy Jeff had seen so often before. Still thin, still ragged. But smiling this time. He didn't hide in the shadows either, but bowed politely at Jeff and returned Jeff's smile.

Funny how much better he looks now, Jeff thought. He bowed slightly, folded his hands in front of his chest in the Chinese way, and said "syeh-syeh." It was Chinese for "thank you". It sounded funny to hear himself speaking another language. He tried it again. He hadn't learned much Chinese — just a few important phrases — but he could at least say thank you. "Syeh-syeh," he repeated. "Thanks a lot."

Wu Liang began chattering and smiling. Jeff didn't have a clue what he was saying but he smiled broadly and nodded like he understood.

"He say he want to stay here. He work for us and learn the Christian teaching," Mr Tsiu translated. "He say he like Christians."

It was later that day that Duncan stopped to talk. He was coughing and tired.

"You're beat. You'd better try to get some rest," Jeff told him.

"Aye, I will. When you are all safe here I'll go and meet my fiancée and bring her up country, and then I'll get back to Nanjing and a less dramatic scene!"

"When are you going to get married?"

Duncan coughed again and wiped perspiration from his forehead before he spoke. "September 25. It seems like an eternity, but it'll not be long when she gets busy with her language study."

He sat down and stretched his long legs out in front of him. "I'm to have a helper until then anyway. D'you know your friend Wu Liang is coming to Nanjing to live with me?"

"No, really? That'll be great. He can help you in lots of ways and you can teach him."

"Right. He trusts us foreigners now. Maybe eventually he'll come to trust our God too."

Jeff sat on the pavement in the courtyard after Duncan left him, arms around his knees, watching Maria and the children. Bertie came running over and sat beside him.

"Jeffrey, are you sad?"

"Who, me? No. I'm not sad. Why?"

"You look sad. Don't be. We're going away for a little while, but Papa says we will come back home again as soon as God lets us. Will you come with us, Jeffrey?"

"I don't know. I guess. I don't know what else I can do." He closed his eyes, and rested his head on his arms. The sun felt warm on his head and back. He was feeling a little dizzy. Sort of like he was drifting off in all directions at once.

Probably from getting hit with the brick last night. That and being tired. He felt the cut on the left side of his head. Still sore, but a scab seemed to be forming.

"Jeffrey." It was Bertie. *Persistent little kid*, Jeff thought. His little hand beat on Jeff's back. "Jeffrey."

"What?" Jeff muttered without lifting his head.

"Are you sick? Did you get hurt last night?"

"No, I'm not sick. Just a bit dizzy. I just got hit on the head a little, nothing serious. Why don't you run off and play for a while. I'll talk to you later. OK?"

He heard the footsteps receding in the distance. There were so many things going around in his mind right now, he couldn't talk to Bertie. But he had to admit he had grown to love the kid. He was just like a little brother. In fact everyone here had become like his family. He was sorry he couldn't help them more. After all, they'd taken him in and given him everything they had during the past few months. He must find Mr Taylor and Maria and thank them.

Hey, he thought suddenly. *I did help. That kid would never have been friendly to foreigners, any more than the others are, if it hadn't been for me saving his life. I made a friend out of him and that helped the whole bunch of us. Maybe even helped the missionaries in other places in the future. I did do something!*

"God, thanks," he said silently. "Thanks for helping me make friends of that kid instead of hating him. And thanks especially for saving our lives last night when we could all have been killed. And thanks for ... well, thanks for all the things I never bothered to thank you for before. Things like good food, and a safe country and a house without holes in the walls, and freedom to walk down the street without being stared at, and Mom and Dad and ... "

His head whirled. He couldn't think straight. What was the matter with him? The hit on the head was over 24 hours ago. Should be over it by now. He had to shake this off so he could help everyone pack. Had to ... his mind went blank. A spell of intense dizziness washed over him. He closed his eyes, hoping the strange sensation would pass.

Someone was helping him up. He opened his eyes and blinked at the white glare of a fluorescent light overhead. Lights in the ceiling. There were no electric lights in China.

Slowly his mind cleared and he pulled himself to a sitting position. A crowd was standing around. Not a Chinese crowd.

"Jeff, are you all right?" It was his mother, rushing over to take his arm. "Are you OK?"

He stood up slowly. Uncle Zeke was fiddling with a maze of buttons and cords on a shattered cockpit. "Blew the thing apart. Never imagined such a thing."

Everyone was talking at once.

"From the looks of it," Zeke was saying, "they didn't get the GDS fixed after all. It shorted out. Look here, Nat." He held a burnt piece of wiring in his hand. "Shorted out. Didn't adjust the GDS like it should have. Just turned it on full blast and blew this door off." The warped metal door lay in the far corner of the room, obviously blown there by a powerful explosion.

"Get a force that strong, it'll just ... just ... well, who knows what it will do to the human body," he said, frowning.

Jeff listened to the explanations, the apologies, the questions. "How did I get back here anyway, I'd like to know."

"Well, as soon as the door blew off of course I reached in and grabbed the lever and stopped the thing. But what d'you mean 'get back here'? You weren't gone anywhere."

"I wasn't?"

"No. Just lying over there on the floor for a few seconds. You blacked out, that's all."

"And scared us half to death," his mother added.

"I guess it was a dream, then. I thought ..." He wanted to say he'd had the exotic adventure he'd hoped for. He caught his mother glancing at him anxiously. Better not to say anything about that.

"Come on, Mom and Dad, let's go. We've s

the experiment. Enough touring of labs."

"Do you think we should have a doctor look at him? I mean, he seems to be confused. This thinking he was away somewhere ..."

"Nah, he'll be all right. Just stunned for a moment, that's all."

Jeff lagged behind his parents as they walked down the hall toward the elevator. What had happened anyway? Had it all been some complicated dream, some kind of hallucination? Hard to believe that, and yet ... He put one hand up gingerly to the left side of his head and ear. It was sore. His fingers ran along a new, soft zee-shaped wound. A smile spread over his face and he nodded slowly.

"Hey, Mom, can we get something to eat, I'm hungry."

Epilog

The Yangzhou riots of 1868 are history. It was a long time before things were peaceful again in that city, but eventually a church was established and CIM missionaries lived there for many years.

Just after the riot, Maria's seventh baby was born — Charles Edward. And two years later, the last, Noel, who died after three weeks. Maria herself died at that time, in July, 1870.

Bertie (Herbert Hudson) was to grow up and have nine children of his own. In fact, his grandson is also a missionary in Asia.

George Duncan and Catherine were married as planned, but in just five years Duncan died of TB.

Hudson Taylor lived to see his dream fulfilled, missionaries living in every province of China.

He died in China July 3, 1905. In time the CIM became the largest mission in China.

The mission Hudson Taylor started is still at work. You'll find it, not in China now, but in the other countries of East Asia, under the name Overseas Missionary Fellowship. Today in places like the Philippines, Taiwan and Indonesia, its missionaries still try to live as much as possible like the people around them, so they can tell them about the Lord Jesus. They still depend on God to provide what they need — and He still does. If you want to know more about OMF, or about Hudson Taylor, write to the address nearest you in the list at the beginning of this book.

Don't miss the second in this series, where Jeff's time travel lands him in an avalanche and leads him face to face with an armed enemy in *East of the Misty Mountains*.